Jobs, Income, and Work

Ruinous Trends, Urgent Alternatives

Holly Sklar

A report for the
Community Relations Division
American Friends Service Committee

1995

This report was published by the Community Relations Division of the
American Friends Service Committee.

March 1995

ISBN 0-910082-29-4

Contents

Preface

According to conventional economic measures, 1994 was a year of economic recovery, vigorous enough to prompt the Federal Reserve to raise interest rates six times in order to slow growth. 1994 was also a turning point. Despite these seemingly upbeat growth statistics, the mood of the voting public was grim and in the November elections, Democratic control in Congress and many state governments was broken. The Republicans were swept to power in an expression of fear, insecurity, resentment, and bigotry. These sentiments make fertile ground for right wing prescriptions that scapegoat those who are poor, or non-White, non-male, non-heterosexual, or not "American."

Where does this fear and anger come from? What are the economic and social events that have produced them? This publication addresses these questions. It traces the ruinous trends in our society towards greater inequality in job opportunities, wages, wealth, ownership, and access to basic services; a curtailment of democracy through decreasing corporate accountability and the ever-increasing power of the corporations and private finance to dictate terms to states as well as nations; the intensification of punitive responses such as welfare cuts, prison expansion, and more severe sentencing; and the scapegoating of people living on the edge while rewarding the wealthy.

Fears about the economy—jobs and income in particular—are certainly one source of the scapegoating. Behind the anti-immigrant legislation in California are the fears of households who feel economically insecure. Behind the attack on welfare mothers are the frustrations and resentments of people who feel overworked, underpaid, and fearful of losing their jobs. Behind the homelessness crisis are the speculative frenzies and the bad bets of the real estate market, yet the blame is heaped on the homeless victims who are increasingly being criminalized.

The American Friends Service Committee (AFSC) has a long history of work relating to economic justice, including support of labor, women's rights, welfare, and civil rights organizing; job creation projects in poor communities; and development of housing for low-income and homeless people. The current focus on the issues of jobs, income, and work grew out of discussions within AFSC's Economic Justice Task Force and the Nationwide Women's Program about welfare reform, particularly the various welfare-to-work proposals. In addition to deploring the principle of a blanket requirement for welfare recipients to work off their benefits, it became clear to us that most welfare-to-work proposals are also impracticable due to an absolute inadequacy in the number of jobs available to welfare recipients, and an even greater shortfall of jobs that pay a liveable wage.

Eva Gladstein, a long-time AFSC committee member, wrote an excellent piece of research and analysis entitled *Livelihoods in Jeopardy*. That title reflects our concerns about falling wages and the lack of job opportunities, as well as our concerns about work that is unpaid and therefore unrecognized. This kind of invisible work includes housework, raising children, caring for the sick, elderly and disabled, and community work. *Jobs, Income, and Work* continues to deepen and broaden our analysis of these issues.

What are the implications of this analysis for AFSC's work? It is striking how far we've traveled—backwards—from the proposal for economic rights by President Roosevelt in 1944 and the UN Declaration of Human Rights in 1948: the right to a job, the right to a decent income, the right to leisure, the right to decent housing, education, and medical care. The conservative agenda that is ascendant today is grounded in the assumption that it is only by denying people these rights that the United States can be competitive and strong. The corporate competitive road is paved with lower wages, fewer benefits, longer hours, union busting, and fewer regulatory "burdens" such as health, safety, and environmental protections. It will be a challenge, in this reactionary climate, simply to re-legitimize the notion of basic economic rights.

And yet the public is not as vengeful as the right wing demagogues would have us believe. The Center for the Study of Policy Attitudes in Washington, D.C. found that 84 percent of the public feels that "society has a moral obligation to try to alleviate poverty." In 1964, 70 percent of the public believed that "government has a responsibility to try to do away with poverty" compared to 80 percent today. So, the "American people" are not fundamentally more mean-spirited than ever before, but they are angry scared, and frustrated. There is a call for change and the only clear vision that is being effectively promoted is that of the right wing agenda.

So what can be done? How can we build a future that reflects a progressive vision of society—a society based on inclusiveness, tolerance, social and economic equality, democratic participation, economic security, and sustainability? There is no single blueprint and, given our commitment to bottom-up organizing, even if there were one we wouldn't want it. On the one hand, progressives are fighting a defensive battle to preserve the shredding safety net. This fight must continue. AFSC will carry on our long tradition of joining and supporting the movements of poor and marginalized people to redress social and economic inequities.

On the other hand there are also efforts to create new institutions, and alternative models of community economic development. There is a lot of exciting work going on at the grassroots level as well as at the national and international levels, including many AFSC programs.

Financial institutions and capital

Community activists have long been aware of the pivotal role of capital in their communities and the degeneration that results from disinvestment and redlining. In New Hampshire, AFSC is working with communities to use the Community Reinvestment Act (CRA) to force banks to fulfill their legal obligation to reinvest in the neighborhoods from which they get deposits.

Communities are setting up their own financial institutions such as credit unions, revolving loan funds, and community investment funds. The purpose is to create institutions that are responsive to the needs of community members rather than strict profit-making criteria. In upstate New York there has been discussion of forming a Youth Credit Union for low-income youth and in New Hampshire, AFSC staff have been active in the N.H. Community Loan Fund.

People are even creating their own money. In Northeast Ohio AFSC has helped to develop a system of local currency in which people can use their talents and skills to barter or buy other local goods and services.

Jobs: retention, creation, and income generation

When the Shenango foundry in western Pennsylvania threatened to close down, the workers and the community struggled through tremendous obstacles to buy out the plant, resulting in the retention of 85 jobs this year and an anticipated 150 by next year. Labor and community groups are becoming increasingly aware of the benefits of working together; throughout the country, labor-community groups have prevented plant closings, promoted worker buyouts, elected progressive candidates, and raised awareness around environmental issues.

In addition to retaining existing jobs, many communities are involved in job creation. In upstate New York, AFSC has been involved in building CommonWorks, a network of cooperatives, and has also engaged in public education about cooperative economic alternatives. In Chicago, youth have become involved in small scale businesses. Native Americans have set up an aquaculture farm and black ash project on the New York Akwesasne reservation. In California AFSC sponsored a "teaching farm" where small farmers learn the basics of growing produce organically.

Workers' Rights

AFSC has been involved in cross-border work helping to publicize corporate abuses of workers and the environment; educating women maquiladora workers about their legal rights and how to use them. In California AFSC has had a long history of working with the farmworkers to organize and improve working conditions, and in West Virginia AFSC was deeply involved in the Pittston mineworkers strike. The Women and Global Corporations Project has challenged the human cost of corporate power both by addressing exploitative policies and providing practical support and solidarity to action alerts and publications.

Housing

AFSC has been involved in housing work for over sixty years, beginning with the construction by coal miners of their own homes in Pennsylvania. In the 1960s, AFSC's organizing in rural areas helped farm workers build their own housing in California and Florida. In Oakland, AFSC worked with Dignity Housing West, an organization of homeless people, to develop permanent housing for homeless people, which has resulted in employment creation including construction, administration, and property management jobs. In Stockton, California, AFSC helped a group of Cambodian families buy out the apartment complex they were living in.

Education

There is a great popular demand for economic literacy. Activists from various backgrounds have come up against the need to understand how the economy affects the issues that they are working on. Certainly this document demystifies many of these issues. AFSC is also continuing to develop trainings in economic literacy and popular education, with a particular emphasis on how women are affected.

Clearly, much crucial work is already underway. However, too often these efforts are isolated from each other and from a broader analysis of how they all fit together. The challenge that we face is to put the many inspirational pieces together to build the hope that there is another way—a coherent alternative to the profit-grubbing, individualistic, overly competitive, market-driven, atomistic, alienating system that we live in.

—Emily Kawano
Community Relations Division
American Friends Service Committee

Introduction: "Chaos or Community?"

The time has come for us to civilize ourselves by the total, direct, and immediate abolition of poverty. . .

A true revolution of values will soon cause us to question the fairness and justice of many of our past and present policies. We are called to play the good Samaritan on life's roadside; but. . . One day the whole Jericho road must be transformed so that men and women will not be beaten and robbed as they make their journey through life. True compassion is more than flinging a coin to a beggar; it understands that an edifice which produces beggars needs restructuring.

A true revolution of values will soon look uneasily on the glaring contrast of poverty and wealth. With righteous indignation, it will look at thousands of working people displaced from their jobs with reduced incomes as a result of automation while the profits of the employers remain intact, and say "This is not just". . .

America, the richest and most powerful nation in the world, can well lead the way in this revolution of values. There is nothing to prevent us from paying adequate wages to schoolteachers. . . There is nothing but a lack of social vision to prevent us from paying an adequate wage to every American citizen whether he be a hospital worker, laundry worker, maid, or day laborer. There is nothing except shortsightedness to prevent us from guaranteeing an annual minimum—and livable—income for every American family. There is nothing, except a tragic death wish, to prevent us from reordering our priorities, so that the pursuit of peace will take precedence over the pursuit of war. There is nothing to keep us from remolding a recalcitrant status quo with bruised hands until we have fashioned it into a brotherhood. . .

The oceans of history are made turbulent by the ever-rising tides of hate. History is cluttered with the wreckage of nations and individuals who pursued this self-defeating path of hate. . .

We are now faced with the fact that tomorrow is today. . . We still have a choice today: nonviolent coexistence or violent coannihilation. This may well be mankind's last chance to choose between chaos and community.

—Martin Luther King Jr.,
Where Do We Go From Here: Chaos or Community? (1967)

Martin Luther King's call is more urgent than ever. In the last quarter-century, humankind has taken giant steps toward community—and chaos. Since 1967, the trends King warned us about have intensified. The "War on Poverty" has given way to the rollback of welfare. Joblessness remains high whether the economy is in recession or "recovery." Real wages for average workers have plummeted. Income inequality is growing. Wealth is being redistributed *upward*. For more and more people, a job is not a ticket out of poverty, but into the ranks of the working poor. Full-time jobs are growing scarcer in the "leaner, meaner" world of global corporate restructuring.

Workers are increasingly expected to migrate from job to job, at low and variable wage rates, without paid vacation, much less a pension. How can they care for themselves and their families, maintain a home, pay for college, save for retirement, or plan a future? How do we build community? What about the millions of people without jobs? This brand of economics is a prescription for chaos.

As real anger rises over these ruinous economic trends, blame is deflected with racist, sexist, homophobic, and xenophobic scapegoating. People who should be working together to transform the economic policies that are hurting them are instead turning hatefully on each other. The shrinking middle class is misled into thinking those below them on the economic ladder are pulling them down, when in reality those on top are rising at the expense of those below. Instead of full employment, the United States has full prisons. The military budget continues to wage the Cold War, while programs to prevent violence and invest in people and the environment are sacrificed on the altar of deficit reduction.[1]

To choose community over chaos we must revitalize democracy with plain talk about who benefits and who loses from government policy. We need vigorous debate over how to reshape policy in the public interest—not the pseudo-debate of false campaign promises, negative political ads, and talk radio hate-mongering. The U.S. economy "fosters inequality," says Eva Gladstein, chair of the Economic Justice Task Force of the American Friends Service Committee (AFSC) Community Relations Division. It accommodates "wages which are not sufficient to meet basic needs. Rather than seek full employment, our economic policies define acceptable levels of unemployment." Acceptable, that is, to corporate elites who undemocratically determine economic policy for the rest of us.

Rights and "entitlements" taken for granted today—among them the eight-hour day, minimum wage, Social Security, and the right of workers to organize and bargain collectively—were obtained in the face of strong opposition. Many of these achievements are being eroded. Demagoguery is threatening democracy. To realize community over chaos we must struggle not only to protect old gains, but forge crucial social and economic rights for the 21st century.

In the words of the United Nations Children's Fund (UNICEF) 1994 report, *The Progress of Nations*:

> The day will come when the progress of nations will be judged not by their military or economic strength, nor by the splendor of their capital cities and public buildings, but by the well-being of their peoples; by their levels of health, nutrition, and education; by their opportunities to earn a fair reward for their labors; by their ability to participate in the decisions that affect their lives; by the respect that is shown for their civil and political liberties; by the provision that is made for those who are vulnerable and disadvantaged; and by the protection that is afforded to the growing minds and bodies of their children.

The progress of nations—of people—will also be judged by the care given to their environment, the lifeblood of generations to come.

Reverse Redistribution

One out of four children is born into poverty in the United States, according to the official measure (see tables 5 and 8). Meanwhile, the combined wealth of the top 1 percent of U.S. families is about the same as that of the entire bottom 95 percent (see table 2). Such inequality befits an oligarchy, not a democracy.

Wealth is being redistributed upward. Between 1977 and 1989, the top 1 percent of families more than doubled their after-tax incomes, adjusting for inflation, while the bottom 60 percent of families lost income (see table 3). Over the 1962 to 1989 period, "roughly three-fourths of new wealth was generated by increasing the value of initial wealth (much of it inherited)." The wealthiest 1 percent owned more than half of all bonds, trusts and business equity; nearly half of all stocks; and 40 percent of non-home real estate in 1989. The bottom 90 percent owned about a tenth of all those assets, except for non-home real estate, of which they owned 20 percent. Not surprisingly, the gap between Whites and people of color is much wider in wealth than income. While the average income of families of color was 63 percent that of White families in 1989, their average wealth (measured by the net worth of assets minus debt) was only 29 percent.[2]

Paycheck inequality has grown so much that the top 4 percent earn more in wages and salaries than the entire bottom half. Back in the booming 1950s, the gap was not as wide: the top 4 percent made as much as the bottom 35 percent in 1959.[3] The average chief executive officer (CEO) of a large corporation has seen pay skyrocket to millions of dollars in salary, bonuses, stock options, and dividends.

The average CEO "earned" as much as 41 factory workers in 1960, 42 factory workers in 1980, 104 factory workers in 1991, and 157 factory workers in 1992 (see table 1). "The disparity tears at the social fabric," observes *Business Week*. The United States leads major industrialized nations with the largest gap between CEO and worker pay. Japan's average CEO, for example, earns less than 32 factory workers. Between 1980 and 1993, U.S. CEO pay increased by 514 percent, workers' wages by 68 percent, consumer prices by 75 percent, and corporate profits by 166 percent.[4] Workers' wages fell way behind inflation. CEO pay zoomed ahead. Yet, CEOs want us to think the problem is overpaid workers.

In 1993, Disney chair Michael Eisner broke CEO compensation records with $203 million. As *Business Week* noted, his pay that year was "nearly equal to the GNP of Grenada." Eisner "didn't bring about Disney's comeback single-handedly. It took the help of thousands of employees, from the people who keep Disney's theme parks clean to the artists in its animation studios. Yet, Eisner and a few members of his senior management team have reaped most of the rewards," says *Business Week.*

"That may make Eisner the best example yet of what economist Robert H. Frank calls a 'winner-take-all' market, in which only a handful of top performers walk away with the lion's share." In 1974, CEOs made 35 times the average salary inside their own company. Today they make about 150 times the average.[5] And thanks to tax changes discussed later, average workers are paying more to the government, while CEOs and their companies are paying less.

On top of their pay packages, CEOs commonly enjoy perks such as gourmet dining, chauffeured limousines, corporate jets, luxury hotels, company-paid residences, vacation retreats, country club and health club memberships, and personal financial and legal advice—as well as signing bonuses at the beginning of their tenures and golden parachutes at the end. In the words of longtime compensation consultant Graef Crystal, the modern CEO is pampered and "paid so much more than ordinary workers that he hasn't got the slightest clue as to how the rest of the country lives." The result is more companies "in search of excess," not excellence. Crystal writes:

> CEOs and other senior executives in the United States earn far more than their counterparts in the other major industrialized countries. And they pay the least taxes. . . By contrast, Japan, the country that gives the United States the greatest competitive fit, pays its CEOs the least, and has the most egalitarian approach to compensation. . .
>
> Is there a lesson here?[6]

Table 1: The CEO-Worker Pay Gap
Annual Average Pay
not adjusted for inflation*

	1960	1970	1980	1992
CEO	190,383	548,787	624,996	3,842,247
Factory Worker	4,665	6,933	15,008	24,411
Teacher	4,995	8,626	15,970	34,098
Engineer	9,828	14,695	28,486	58,240
CEO multiple of factory worker pay	41	79	42	157

*As seen in other tables, inflation-adjusted worker pay is falling.
Source: *Business Week*, April 26, 1993.

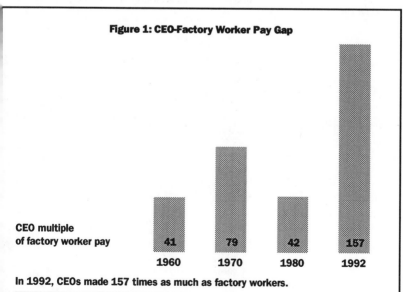

Figure 1: CEO-Factory Worker Pay Gap

CEO multiple
of factory worker pay

| 41 | 79 | 42 | 157 |
| 1960 | 1970 | 1980 | 1992 |

In 1992, CEOs made 157 times as much as factory workers.

Source: *Business Week*, April 26, 1993.

Table 2
Percent Distribution of Household Wealth and Income, 1989

Share of Households	Net Worth (assets minus debt)	Household Income	Financial Net Wealth (net worth minus net equity in owner-occupied housing)
Top 1%	38.9	16.4	48.1
Bottom 90%	27.6	60.0	16.2
Bottom 95%	39.1	70.5	27.7
Top 0.5%	31.4	13.4	39.3
Next 0.5%	7.5	3.0	8.8
Next 4.0%	21.9	13.3	24.1
Next 5.0%	11.5	10.5	11.5
Next 10.0%	12.2	15.5	10.1
Bottom 80.0%	15.4	44.5	6.1
Top Fifth	84.6	55.5	93.9
Upper Middle Fifth	11.5	20.7	6.8
Middle Fifth	4.6	13.2	1.5
Lower Middle Fifth	0.8	7.6	0.1
Bottom Fifth	−1.4	3.1	−2.3

Source: Edward N. Wolff, "Trends in Household Wealth in the United States, 1962–83 and 1983–89," *Review of Income and Wealth*, June 1994, Table 4. Also see, "The Rich Get Increasingly Richer: Latest Data on Household Wealth During the 1980s," Economic Policy Institute, *Briefing Paper*, 1992, Table 2. Wolff explains differences with Census data, which understates income and wealth at the top.

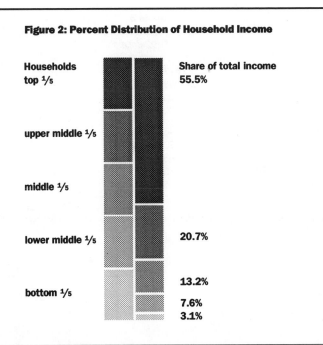

Figure 2: Percent Distribution of Household Income

Households
top ⅕

upper middle ⅕

middle ⅕

lower middle ⅕

bottom ⅕

Share of total income
55.5%

20.7%

13.2%
7.6%
3.1%

Source: Edward N. Wolff, "Trends in Household Wealth in the United States, 1962–83 and 1983–89," *Review of Income and Wealth*, June 1994, Table 4. Also see, "The Rich Get Increasingly Richer: Latest Data on Household Wealth During the 1980s," Economic Policy Institute, *Briefing Paper*, 1992, Table 2. Wolff explains differences with Census data, which understates income and wealth at the top.

Table 3
Changes in Average After-Tax Family Income, 1977–89
in 1992 dollars

	1977	1989	% Change
Overall	30,948	33,663	+8.8
Top 1%	202,809	410,148	+102.2
Top 5%	103,760	158,347	+52.6
Top Fifth	63,546	81,399	+28.1
Upper Middle Fifth	36,563	37,379	+2.2
Middle Fifth	27,788	26,350	−5.2
Lower Middle Fifth	18,885	16,987	−10.0
Bottom Fifth	8,495	7,608	−10.4

Source: U.S. House of Representatives, Committee on Ways and Means, Subcommittee on Human Resources, *Background Material on Family Income and Benefit Changes* (December 19, 1991), p. 68.

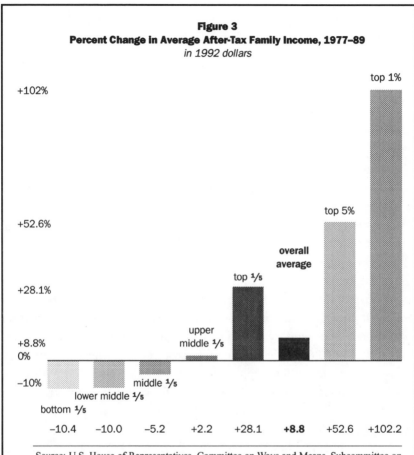

Figure 3
Percent Change in Average After-Tax Family Income, 1977–89
in 1992 dollars

Source: U.S. House of Representatives, Committee on Ways and Means, Subcommittee on Human Resources, *Background Material on Family Income and Benefit Changes* (December 19, 1991), p. 68.

Persistent Impoverishment

For many in the United States, there is an endless Great Depression. It's covered up with scapegoating terms like "underclass" and Orwellian ones like "jobless recovery," and by officially undercounting the unemployed and impoverished.

The official poverty line understates the real extent of poverty, especially among the working poor. Poverty rates would be much higher if the official measure reflected the actual cost of living and after-tax income. The official poverty line was established in the 1960s by determining the cost of a minimally adequate diet and multiplying by three, assuming then that the average family spent one-third of its budget on food (the food plan underlying the poverty line assumed that households baked daily and cooked everything from scratch, and it was meant to be nutritionally adequate only under temporary or emergency conditions). The government has not adjusted the poverty formula to reflect the current cost of food, which is now much lower in relation to housing, health care, and other necessities. It simply takes the previous year's poverty line (specific poverty thresholds are set for different size households), based on an increasingly inadequate formula, and adjusts it for inflation.

"Many poor families," observes the Children's Defense Fund, "manage by cutting back on food, jeopardizing their health and the development of their children, or by living in substandard and sometimes dangerous housing. Some do without heat, electricity, telephone service, or plumbing for months or years. Many do without health insurance, health care, safe child care, or reliable transportation to take them to and from work. Confronted with impossible choices and inadequate basics, and lacking any cushion of savings or assets. . . many are just one illness, job loss, or family crisis away from homelessness or family dissolution."[7] Impoverished two-parent White or Black families are about twice as likely as nonpoor two-parent families to break up, the U.S. Census Bureau reports. "Stresses arising from low income and poverty may have contributed substantially to discontinuation rates for two-parent families."[8]

In their book on the working poor, John Schwarz and Thomas Volgy show that, based on a stringent economy budget, a family of four needed an income of about 155 percent of the official poverty line to buy minimally sufficient food, housing, health care, transportation, clothing, and other personal and household items, and pay taxes. They warn that their stringent budget does not cover many things, such as paid child care. It does not provide for people who cannot find low-cost housing. Low-income families spend an average one-fourth of their incomes on child care. The gap between low-cost housing units and low-income households is vast; by 1991, there were 4.5 million fewer low-rent units than low-income renters.

Using Schwarz and Volgy's formula, one person in four is living in poverty.[9] By contrast, the official 1993 poverty rate was 15 percent, or one out of seven persons. That's still about 39 million people in the United States (see table 5). Nearly 41 percent of officially poor people were in families whose total incomes were *below half* the respective poverty thresholds.

Some people argue that the official poverty rate overstates poverty because it does not include noncash benefits such as food stamps in measuring income (cash benefits such as Social Security and AFDC are included). However, adjusting for the current cost of necessities has a much greater effect (upward) than the effect (downward) of adding noncash benefits (see table 4). It's also important to note that, contrary to common belief, more than one out of four officially poor people receive *no* government assistance of any kind—cash or noncash. Fewer than one out of five officially poor people live in public or subsidized housing. Half live in households that receive no food stamps. Moreover, according to the Census Bureau, despite the existence of programs such as Medicaid and Medicare, 29 percent of the officially poor had no public or private medical insurance of any kind at any time during 1993. Schwarz and Volgy point out that the issue of whether to include current noncash benefits "largely dissolves if an income significantly above the official poverty line" is recognized as reflecting needed income, because at that level people receive only small amounts, if any, of noncash benefits.[10]

Table 4
Adjusting the Poverty Rate for Food/Housing Costs and Noncash Benefits,
1988

Adjusting for Food Costs	Adjusting for Housing Costs	Official Poverty Rate	Adjusting for Government Food and Housing Benefits
25.8%	23.0%	13.0%	11.6%

Note: Noncash medical benefits are omitted. As the congressional *1993 Green Book* explains, "The development of the poverty thresholds did not take into account medical costs. Although poor persons are clearly better off with medical coverage, such benefits cannot be used by recipients to meet other needs of daily living. Also, since health insurance costs are not imputed to the incomes of those above poverty, it seems inappropriate to count health benefits for those below the poverty line." In the words of Mishel and Bernstein, "their inclusion would have the perverse effect of making the ill appear less poor."
Sources: Mishel and Bernstein, *The State of Working America 1994–95*, pp. 255–56, citing Ruggles (1992); U.S. House Committee on Ways and Means, *1993 Green Book*, pp. 1318–20. 1988 is the latest year of available data for comparison.

When it comes to children, the United States is the poorest of rich nations. A comparison among industrialized democracies showed that U.S. income is the most unevenly distributed and found:

> the child poverty rate in the United States, after taxes and benefits are considered, was more than twice that in Canada and four times the average child poverty rate in the other nations in the study. It also showed that the poverty rate just among White children in the United States was higher than the poverty rate among *all* children in all other countries in the study except Australia. In short, the private economy in the United States generates more relative poverty among children than the private economies of many other western, industrialized nations—and the United States then does far less than the other nations to address this problem.[11]

Though long the world's wealthiest nation, the United States lags behind other industrialized democracies in assuring basic human needs—health care being today's best-known example. All people and communities need services. In higher-income communities, people needing doctors or psychologists, lawyers or drug treatment, tutors or child care, can afford private practitioners and avoid the stigma that unjustly accompanies public social services. In lower-income communities they cannot. Here, though unemployment is high and wages increasingly low, public social services are commonly stingy, humiliating, and punitive. Here, while the income gap is widening and the "safety net" shredded, prisons and other "corrections spending" make up the fastest-growing part of state budgets.[12]

As a consequence of unconscionable poverty and governmental neglect, proportionately more children die before their first birthday in the United States than in 20 other countries. The death rate of Black babies in the United States ranks 35th, tied with Bulgaria and Chile, and behind such nations as Jamaica, Sri Lanka, Poland, Cuba, and Kuwait. In the United States, Black babies are more than twice as likely to die before their first birthday as White babies, and their life expectancy is seven years less.[13]

Table 5
Percent Below Official and Alternative Poverty Levels, 1993

	Official Poverty Line*	150%	175%	50%
			of official poverty line	
All Persons	**15.1**	25.0	30.3	6.9
Men	**13.3**	22.5	27.7	5.4
Women	**16.9**	27.4	32.8	6.9
Children under 18	**22.7**	34.0	39.8	10.1
Related Children under 6	**25.6**	37.6	43.9	11.8
65 Years & over	**12.2**	27.4	35.2	2.4
White	**12.2**	21.3	26.5	4.5
men	**10.7**	19.2	24.1	3.9
women	**13.7**	23.4	28.7	5.0
children under 18	**17.8**	28.3	33.9	6.9
related children under 6	**20.1**	31.6	37.6	7.9
65 years & over	**10.7**	25.1	32.9	2.1
Black	**33.1**	47.2	53.8	16.7
men	**29.7**	42.9	50.0	15.4
women	**36.0**	51.0	57.2	17.8
children under 18	**46.1**	61.2	67.8	26.1
related children under 6	**51.7**	66.9	74.5	30.6
65 years & over	**28.0**	51.1	59.4	5.2
Latino†	**30.6**	48.2	55.5	10.5
men	**27.6**	45.7	53.3	9.0
women	**33.6**	50.9	57.9	12.1
children under 18	**40.9**	60.2	67.3	14.5
related children under 6	**43.4**	62.8	70.0	15.8
65 years & over	**21.4**	44.5	52.3	3.7
Asian & Pacific Islander	**15.3**			
Non-Latino White	**9.9**			
Am. Indian, Eskimo, Aleut, 1990 ‡	**30.9**			
Persons 15 years & over 1991–92				
with no disability	**12.2**	20.5		
with a disability	**19.3**	33.8		
with a severe disability	**24.3**	41.8		

*Official 1993 poverty thresholds: 1 person under 65, $7,518; 1 person 65 & over, $6,930; 2 persons including 1 child under 18: $9,960; 3 persons including 1 child under 18, $11,631; 4 persons including 2 children under 18, $14,654. Alternative measures vary at about 150 to 170 percent of the official poverty line. Data not available in all categories.
†Latinos may be of any race.
‡1990 Census figure from Census Bureau statistician, September 19, 1994. Last year available. Sources: Census Bureau, *Income, Poverty, and Valuation of Noncash Benefits: 1993,* prepublication Table 6, "Age, Sex, Household Relationship, Race, and Hispanic Origin, by Ratio of Income to Poverty Level: 1993"; John M. McNeil, Census Bureau, *Americans With Disabilities: 1991–92,* December 1993, Table 8. On alternative measures, see Schwarz and Volgy, *The Forgotten Americans,* pp. 35–45.

Breakdown of the Paycheck

By the standards of today, the United States offers both cheap energy and cheap labor—and the all-too-rare plus of political stability. . . In Germany, the Netherlands, Belgium, and Sweden, average wages for manufacturing workers now exceed comparable U.S. wages by as much as 20 percent.
—*Business Week*, July 9, 1979.

The standard [of living] of the average American has to decline.
—Federal Reserve Chair Paul Volcker, October 1979.[14]

It is fashionable to blame the supposed "breakdown of the family" for promoting poverty and ignore the breakdown in wages and employment. The scapegoating stereotype of deadbeat poor people masks the growing reality of dead-end jobs and disposable workers. Living standards are falling for younger generations despite the fact that many households have two wage earners, have fewer children, and are better educated than their parents.

The average real (inflation-adjusted) weekly earnings of production and nonsupervisory private sector workers crashed 16 percent between 1973 and 1993—falling below 1967 levels (see table 6). These workers make up more than 80 percent of wage and salary employment. The postwar pattern of upward income mobility was broken, beginning with those born between 1955 and 1964.[15]

The inflation-adjusted median income for young families with children—headed by persons younger than 30—plunged 32 percent between 1973 and 1990. Median income was nearly cut in half for Black families with children headed by persons under 30 (see table 7).

Forty percent of all children in families headed by someone younger than 30 were *officially* living in poverty in 1990, including one out of four children in White young families and one out of five children in young married-couple families[16] (see table 8). Were it not for the increased work hours and earnings of women since 1973, married-couple families would be significantly poorer.

Table 6
Hourly and Weekly Earnings of Production and Nonsupervisory Workers,
1947–93
in 1993 dollars

Year	Average Hourly Earnings	Average Weekly Earnings
1947	6.75	272.16
1967	10.67	405.40
1973	**12.06**	**445.10**
1979	12.03	429.42
1989	11.26	389.50
1991	10.95	375.55
1993	**10.83**	**373.64**
% Change 1973–93	–10.2%	–16.1%

Source: Mishel and Bernstein, *The State of Working America 1994–95*, Table 3.3.

Real wages are dropping because of global corporate restructuring, deunionization, the shift toward lower-paying industries, the lower value of the minimum wage, increased part-time and other contingent work, upsized unemployment and underemployment, automation, and other trends. Falling wages can't be explained by common rationales such as slow productivity growth, higher-cost fringe benefits, or a supposed skills and education deficit. The Economic Policy Institute shows that taking into account health and pension benefits and payroll taxes, the total inflation-adjusted hourly compensation for private sector employees has declined over 8 percent since 1977. Though "the most commonly mentioned reason for recent wage problems is slow productivity growth," the reality is that wages have fallen behind productivity. According to the Economic Policy Institute, productivity "grew a total of 3.6 percent between 1973 and 1979 [0.6 percent annually versus 2.4 percent annually during 1959–73] and another 8.7 percent from 1979 to 1989 [0.8 percent annually]," and it grew at 1.5 percent annually between 1989 and 1992.[17] In 1991, annual productivity growth reached 2.3 percent and, in 1992, nearly 3 percent.[18]

Business Week argues that productivity—output per worker—is significantly undermeasured: "The government has no good way of measuring output in a whole range of industries, including banking, software, legal services, wholesale trade, and communication—all of which have invested heavily in information technology. . . Most economists now believe that productivity growth in these industries is substantially understated by the

Table 7
Median Income of Families with Children Under 18,
Headed by Persons Younger than 30, 1973–90
in 1990 dollars

	1973	1979	1989	1990	% Change 1973–89*	% Change 1973–90
All young families with children	27,765	25,204	20,665	18,844	–25.6	–32.1
Married-couple	30,947	30,496	28,279	27,000	–8.6	–12.8
Male-headed	18,547	16,531	17,907	16,000	–3.5	–13.7
Female-headed	9,962	9,360	7,471	7,256	–25.0	–27.2
White, non-Latino	29,475	28,246	24,858	23,000	–15.7	–22.0
Black, non-Latino	17,958	14,371	11,677	9,286	–35.0	–48.3
Latino	19,704	19,213	16,463	14,200	–16.4	–27.9
Other, non-Latino	25,825	22,336	22,217	15,908	–14.0	–38.4
High School dropout	18,842	16,213	12,543	10,213	–33.4	–45.8
High School graduate	28,410	26,298	21,650	20,000	–23.8	–29.6
Some College	31,710	30,892	26,666	27,000	–15.9	–14.9
College graduate	37,757	36,900	42,181	38,700	+11.7	+2.5

*1973, 1979, 1989 were business-cycle peaks with low official unemployment. Author's calculations for % change 1973–89.
Source: Children's Defense Fund, *Vanishing Dreams*, Appendix, Table 3.

government figures. As a result, overall productivity growth for the economy is understated by 'something around the order of one-half to one percentage point a year,' says W. Erwin Diewert, an economist at the University of British Columbia."[19]

Rising productivity in the 1990s, says *Fortune*, demonstrates that the "productivity payoff" from information technology and related corporate reengineering has arrived.[20] There has been no wage payoff for most workers. As *Fortune* observed in 1993:

> If a pat on the back in lieu of a raise can feel like a slap in the face, who dares complain? These days, having a job is a privilege, and keeping it is the measure of success. With raises few and tiny, FedEx couriers have seen their real wages decline by more than 15 percent since 1988. Says compensation director Bill Cahill: "What people are saying is, 'Please, keep me employed.' They're not out there clamoring for a raise."[21]

"Good jobs at good wages" are becoming harder to find and keep. Between 1979 and 1992, the proportion of year-round, full-time workers paid low wages jumped from 12 to 18 percent—nearly one in every five full-

Table 8
Official Poverty Rates Among Children in Families
Headed by Persons Younger than 30
Percent 1973–90

	1973*	1979	1989	1990	% Change 1973–89	% Change 1973–90
All children						
in young families	20.1	23.8	35.0	40.0	74.1	99.0
Married-couple	7.9	10.8	16.5	19.6	108.8	148.1
Male-headed	21.0	22.0	27.8	28.3	32.4	34.8
Female-headed	67.9	61.7	71.2	76.8	4.9	13.1
White, non-Latino	12.1	14.8	23.6	27.2	95.0	124.8
Black, non-Latino	47.4	48.8	59.0	68.4	24.5	44.3
Latino	35.0	36.1	45.2	51.4	29.1	46.9
Other, non-Latino	22.3	33.0	40.6	34.0	82.1	52.5
High School dropout	39.3	44.3	57.9	64.0	47.3	62.8
High School graduate	13.1	19.0	28.4	32.9	116.8	151.1
Some College	8.6	9.6	19.7	21.4	129.0	148.8
College graduate	2.6	4.0	7.3	6.9	180.8	165.4

*1973 was a low point for family poverty rates. Author's calculations for % change, 1973–89.
Source: Children's Defense Fund, *Vanishing Dreams*, Appendix, Table 7.

time workers overall, one out of four women workers, one out of four Black workers, and nearly one out of three Latino workers. Almost half of all young full-time workers, ages 18 to 24, earn low wages, up sharply from 1979 [22] (see table 9). The United States is the only major industrialized nation where low-wage workers have had large declines in real earnings.[23]

The U.S. government has encouraged lower wages and wider income inequality by letting the minimum wage plummet in value. In 1967, a full-time, year-round worker paid minimum wage earned above the official poverty line for a family of three. The same was true in 1979. No longer. By 1993, these wage earners were $647 below the official poverty line for a family of two and $2,442 below the line for a family of three. "Raised 12 times between 1950 and 1981, the [minimum] wage went through a unique dry spell during the 1980s. As prices rose. . . Congress held the wage constant at $3.35," report the authors of *Raising the Floor*. Minimum wage was increased in 1990 to $3.80 and in 1991 to $4.25. But the 1993 value of the minimum wage, adjusting for inflation, is 25 percent less than it was in 1979.

The falling real minimum wage has had an impact well beyond those actually earning the minimum, and an especially hard impact on women, people of color, and rural workers. As *Raising the Floor* puts it, "The minimum wage, often dismissed by policy makers and economists as the social safety net of teenagers and part-time workers, is in fact a key determinant of wages for a significant segment of the U.S. work force—high-school educated workers starting out in the job market." Workers close to the minimum—disproportionately women and people of color—tend to receive raises when the minimum wage goes up. Most minimum wage earners are adults, not teenagers. Two out of three workers who earn minimum wage are women. "Many policy analysts predicted that the 1990 and 1991 changes in the minimum wage would have disastrous effects. . . but economists studying these changes have not found the expected negative trade-off between employment levels and increases in the minimum."[24]

Table 9
Low Earners and High Earners, 1979–92
Percent of year-round, full-time civilian workers ages 16 and over
in 1992 dollars

	Percent with Low Earnings Below $13,091			Percent with High Earnings Above $52,364		
	1979	1992	% change	1979	1992	% change
Men	7.7	14.1	+6.4	15.0	14.7	–0.3
Women	20.4	23.6	+3.2	1.3	3.4	+2.1
Ages 18–24	22.9	47.1	+24.2	na	na	na
Ages 25–34	8.8	18.4	+9.6	na	na	na
White Men	7.2	11.6	+4.4	15.9	16.4	+0.5
White Women	19.8	21.1	+1.3	1.3	3.8	+2.5
Black Men	14.0	19.4	+5.4	4.2	5.1	+0.9
Black Women	24.3	26.9	+2.6	0.5	1.6	+1.1
Latino Men	13.4	26.4	+13.0	5.2	5.3	+0.1
Latina Women	32.3	36.6	+4.3	1.0	1.8	+0.8
No High School Diploma						
Men	15.3	32.2	+16.9	4.7	2.5	–2.2
Women	40.1	54.7	+14.6	0.3	0.4	+0.1
High School Dipl., no college						
Men	7.8	16.7	+8.9	8.9	5.5	–3.4
Women	21.1	30.0	+8.9	0.5	1.1	+0.6
College Bachelor's or higher						
Men	3.1	6.3	+3.2	34.4	33.5	–0.9
Women	7.2	8.5	+1.3	4.2	9.6	+5.4

Source: Census Bureau, "The Earnings Ladder: Who's at the Bottom? Who's at the Top?" *Statistical Brief*, March 1994.

Table 10
Real Hourly Wage and Share of Work Force by Education, 1973–93
in 1993 dollars

Years	H.S. Dropout	H.S. Graduate	Some College	College Graduate	College & 2+ years
Hourly Wages					
1973	10.16	11.63	12.86	16.99	20.91
1979	10.06	11.23	12.24	15.52	18.80
1987	8.74	10.49	11.96	15.98	19.77
1989	8.44	10.21	11.82	15.90	20.36
1990	8.21	10.04	11.81	15.99	20.29
1993	7.87	9.92	11.37	15.71	19.93
% Change					
1973–79	−1.1	−3.5	−4.8	−8.6	−10.1
1979–89	−16.1	−9.1	−3.5	+2.4	+8.3
1989–93	−6.7	−2.8	−3.8	−1.2	−2.1
1973–93	−22.5	−14.7	−11.6	−7.5	−4.7
% Share of Work Force					
1973	28.5	41.8	15.1	8.8	3.6
1989	13.7	40.5	22.3	14.0	6.9
Men's Wages					
1973	11.85	14.02	14.73	19.41	22.20
1979	11.58	13.49	14.29	18.10	20.31
1990	9.23	11.54	13.45	18.16	22.35
1993	8.64	11.19	12.70	17.62	21.71
% Change					
1973–79	−2.3	−3.8	−2.9	−6.7	−8.5
1973–93	−27.1	−20.2	−13.8	−9.2	−2.2
Women's Wages					
1973	7.16	8.79	9.89	13.35	17.36
1979	7.44	8.81	9.67	11.79	15.35
1990	6.59	8.50	10.20	13.52	17.20
1993	6.56	8.57	10.19	13.57	17.69
% Change					
1973–79	+3.9	+0.2	−2.3	−11.6	−11.6
1973–93	−8.4	−2.4	+3.1	+1.7	+1.9

Share of Work force by Highest Degree Attained, 1993*

	Less than High School	High School/ GED	Associate College	College Bachelor's	Masters	Ph.D., law degree, etc.	At least High Sch. degree	At least College Bachelor's
Total	11.1	56.1	8.0	16.9	5.9	2.0	88.9	24.8
Men	13.1	54.5	7.2	16.8	5.8	2.6	86.9	25.2
Women	9.0	57.8	8.9	17.0	6.0	1.3	91.0	24.3

Note: Work force ages 18 and over. 1993 education data different because in 1992 the Census Bureau Current Population Survey changed how it measures educational attainment.
Source: Mishel and Bernstein, *The State of Working America 1994–95*, Tables 3.18–3.21

Lower Wages and Higher Education

A college degree is increasingly necessary, but not necessarily sufficient to earn a decent income. College graduates are also experiencing the wage rollback. But what about the idea that technology-driven demand for more educated or more skilled workers is driving the decline in wages? The real hourly wages for high school graduates dropped 15 percent between 1973 and 1993. Since 1990, college graduates "have been losing ground at the same rate as workers with less education," reports the Economic Policy Institute's *The State of Working America 1994–95*. "By 1993, the wages of these 'more-skilled' workers were. . . 7.5 percent *below* their 1973 level. In other words, although college-educated workers had a wage advantage in the 1980s, the growth in their wage premium during that time reflects not a 'bidding up' of their wages but rather the driving down of the wages of non-college-educated workers." In short, "rather than a 'skill deficit,' working Americans are confronting a 'wage deficit.' " [25]

Note that despite men's wage losses from 1973 to 1993 and small gains by women with more education, male high school graduates still have higher hourly wages than women with some college education, and male college graduates have higher wages than women with graduate education (see table 10). *The State of Working America* predicts that if current trends persist, over the next ten years "the median male wage will fall another 10.4 percent (from $11.24 to $10.07) and the median woman's wage will rise another 4.7 percent (from $8.79 to $9.21). Entry-level wages for high school graduates [the majority of the work force], in this scenario, could be expected to fall another 24 percent among young men (from $6.68 to $5.50), and another 13 percent among young women (from $6.15 to $5.34)." [26]

What about all those supposedly high-paid jobs in high-tech industries requiring higher education? It's important not to confuse the occupations with *high growth rates* with occupations creating the *largest number of jobs* (see table 11). Over half of the total job growth projected over the 1992 to 2005 period will be in occupations that don't require more than a high school education. According to a 1992 Labor Department study, 30 percent of each new class of college "graduates between now and 2005 will march straight into the ranks of the jobless or the underemployed." [27]

Table 11
Projected Jobs 1992–2005
moderate growth scenario
in descending order

Fastest growing occupations by growth rate	Occupations producing the most new jobs
home health aides	retail salespersons
human services workers	registered nurses
personal and home care aides	cashiers
computer engineers and scientists	general office clerks
systems analysts	truck drivers
physical and corrective therapy assistants and aides	waiters and waitresses
physical therapists	nursing aides, orderlies, and attendants
paralegals	janitors and cleaners
special education teachers	food preparation workers
medical assistants	systems analysts
private detectives	home health aides
correction officers	secondary school teachers
child care workers	child care workers
travel agents	guards
radiologic technologists and technicians	marketing and sales worker supervisors

Sources: U.S. Department of Labor, Bureau of Labor Statistics, *The American Work Force: 1992–2005* (April 1994), pp. 72–73. Also see, *1993 Green Book*, p. 539.

Union-Free Labor

Few American managers have ever accepted the right of unions to exist,
even though that's guaranteed by the 1935 Wagner Act. Over the past dozen
years, in fact, U.S. industry has conducted one of the most successful anti-
union wars ever, illegally firing thousands of workers for exercising their
rights to organize.

—*Business Week*, May 23, 1994.

Let there be no doubt: a revitalization of the labor movement would help
reverse the erosion of the middle class.

—Secretary of Labor Robert Reich,
New York Times, August 31, 1994.

Union jobs provide better wages and benefits than their nonunion counterparts, but they are fast disappearing. Union workers earned average weekly
wages of $547 in 1992 compared to $412 for nonunion workers. "In terms
of total compensation, the average union advantage runs a little more than
$14,000 a year. . . The average union advantage in wages alone was 32
percent, or about $7,000 a year. The average union differential has remained
in the 30 to 35 percent range for the past decade." Unions have the greatest
effect in raising the wages of lower-wage workers.[28]

Since the mid-1970s, employers have won a majority of National Labor
Relations Board (NLRB) elections. "A number of studies indicate that management opposition to unions, particularly illegal campaign tactics, is a
major, if not the major, determinant of NLRB election results." [29]

The federal government sent a clear union-busting signal to employers
when President Reagan fired the striking air controllers. According to an
analysis of NLRB figures by University of Chicago professors Rober
LaLonde and Bernard Meltzer, cited in *Business Week*, "employers illegally
fired 1 of every 36 union supporters during organizing drives in the late
1980s, versus 1 in 110 in the late 1970s and 1 in 209 in the late 1960s .
Unlawful firings occurred in one-third of all representation elections in the
late 1980s, versus 8 percent in the late 1960s . . 'Even more significant that

the numbers is the perception of risk among workers, who think they'll be fired in an organizing campaign,' says Harvard law professor Paul C. Weiler. Indeed, when managements obey the law, they don't defeat unions nearly as often." [30] Strike activity has reached record lows. In 1992, there were only 35 strikes involving 1,000 or more workers, versus a peak of 424 such strikes in 1974.[31]

Union votes were important to Bill Clinton's election as president, but Clinton did not deliver on his promises. The passage of the North American Free Trade Agreement (NAFTA), which unions opposed, was followed by the defeat of legislation banning permanent striker replacements, which unions supported. Referring to the striker replacement ban, right wing commentator George Will observes, "Even with a Democratic president, organized labor's highest priority was flicked away like a nettlesome gnat." [32]

The percentage of the work force that is unionized has declined sharply from a peak of over 35 percent in 1945, to under 16 percent in 1994. While public sector unionization has grown to nearly 37 percent, the Labor Research Association predicts that private sector unionization, 11.5 percent in 1992, "will sink to 5 percent by the end of the decade unless labor laws are reformed and unions commit more resources to organizing." [33]

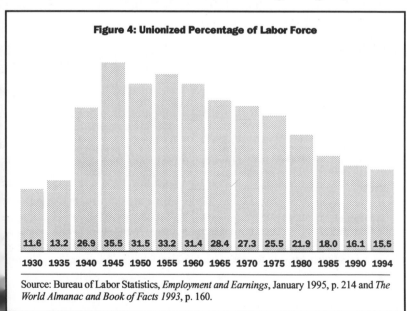

Figure 4: Unionized Percentage of Labor Force

11.6	13.2	26.9	35.5	31.5	33.2	31.4	28.4	27.3	25.5	21.9	18.0	16.1	15.5
1930	1935	1940	1945	1950	1955	1960	1965	1970	1975	1980	1985	1990	1994

Source: Bureau of Labor Statistics, *Employment and Earnings*, January 1995, p. 214 and *The World Almanac and Book of Facts 1993*, p. 160.

In an article supporting corporatist-style unions, *Business Week* acknowledges the link between declining union membership, on the one hand, and lower wages and benefits and widening income disparities on the other: "The resulting drag on pay for millions of people accounts for at least 20 percent of the widening gap between rich and poor," and weakening unions are "a key reason for the six-percentage-point slide in the 1980s in the share of employees with company pension plans, for the seven-point decline in those with employer health plans, and for a 125-fold explosion in unlawful-discharge suits now that fewer employees have a union to stick up for them."

"Unions are often blamed for more trouble than they've caused," *Business Week* adds. "In the 1970s, for instance, many executives believed that unions inflated prices by lifting wages above some presumed market level. Since then, however, more than 50 quantitative studies have concluded that the higher productivity of unionized companies offsets most of their higher costs." [34]

U.S. workers work longer for less than do more unionized workers of other major industrialized countries. As the U.S. Commission on the Future of Worker-Management Relations acknowledges, "The U.S. earnings distribution among workers has widened greatly and is the most unequal among" industrialized countries. Meanwhile, U.S. workers put in about 200 more hours per year than West European workers. A major cause is the difference in vacation time. "Americans with sufficient seniority typically get two weeks of vacation, though some get more and others less. By contrast, Europeans typically obtain four to five week vacations, often legally mandated, from the first year hired." [35] In the words of the *American Labor Yearbook*:

> With the possible exception of Hong Kong and South Korea, the United States provides workers with less legal protection than any other industrialized country. . . [It] has the smallest proportion of workers covered by collective bargaining agreements.
>
> The United States has become a cheap labor haven for global capital looking for low wage and benefit costs, high productivity, and a nonunion environment. . . For example, German firms such as BMW, Adidas, Siemens, and Mercedes are moving into the Carolinas, where huge tax breaks are available and the unionization rate is below 5 percent. [36]

Disposable Workers

The jobs of today and tomorrow not only pay less than the disappearing unionized jobs; they are much more exploitative and precarious. More workers are going back to a future of sweatshops and migrant labor. Corporations are rapidly replacing full-time jobs with variations on day labor and piece work. It's a global trend that is hurting workers around the world.

As the *American Labor Yearbook* sums it up, "The dominant trend in the corporate world is the modular corporation—companies that focus all their energy on a few core activities and outsource everything else. Companies are shedding plants and workers and operating with a network of suppliers held together by temporary agreements. A 'core' group of permanent employees handle the core activities, and contractors or contingent workers are used to manage surges in demand or to handle special projects or noncore needs. An important part of the modular style is to stay union-free to avoid any restrictive work rules or job security arrangements."[37]

This is "the age of the contingent or temporary worker, of the consultant and subcontractor, of the just-in-time work force—fluid, flexible, disposable," writes Lance Morrow in *Time* magazine. "Companies are portable, workers are throwaway."[38] It is the age of "McJobs."

Contingent workers are temporary workers, contract workers, "leased" employees, and part-time workers, a growing share of them involuntary part-timers wanting permanent full-time work. Contingent workers made up a third of the U.S. work force in 1993, up sharply from one-fourth in 1988. Some full-time workers are finding themselves fired and then "leased" back at a large discount by the same companies.[39] The Milwaukee-based temporary agency, Manpower Inc., has become the largest employer in the United States. Manpower's CEO estimates that two-thirds of his work force would rather be working in permanent positions. In 1993, the Michigan electronics manufacturer Robertshaw Controls opened a factory staffed entirely with Manpower temps.[40]

Contingent workers are expected to *outnumber* permanent full-time employees by the end of the decade. More than three-quarters of all the new net jobs from 1979 to 1989 were in the low-paying retail trade and services (business, personnel, health) industries, which employ a large share of part-timers. Between March 1991, the official end of the last recession, and July 1993, more than a quarter of the new jobs were provided by temporary help agencies and another quarter were part-time jobs, three-quarters of which were filled by involuntary part-timers. "An incredible 60 percent of the 1,230,000 jobs created between January and July 1993 were part-time jobs, with half of these part-time jobs filled by people wanting full-time jobs. Another 241,000 (20 percent) of the new jobs were people becoming self-employed—a category that includes underemployed people making do with makeshift work as well as budding entrepreneurs."[41] The number of involuntary part-timers has almost tripled since 1970, reaching 6.3 million people in 1993.[42] Male part-timers earned 41 percent less per hour than full-time workers in 1989. Women part-timers earned 24 percent less in wages per hour than women working full-time. The compensation difference was even greater in terms of health insurance and other benefits. The average weekly income of full-time workers in 1992 was $445, while it was $259 for temporary workers, and $132 for part-time workers, growing numbers of whom don't have the opportunity to work full-time.[43]

Besides lower wages, scarcer benefits, and poorer prospects for promotion, contingent workers are excluded or penalized by current labor law, Social Security, disability, and unemployment compensation. For example, the majority of states exclude part-time workers and independent contractors from the unemployment insurance program. When the New Deal-era Social Security and unemployment programs were established, the occupations excluded from coverage, such as private domestic workers and agricultural laborers, were ones with large numbers of women and people of color. They got a raw deal that lasted for generations. Domestic workers became entitled to Social Security pensions in 1951, but received virtually no unemployment protection until 1978, when federal law required coverage of certain farm workers and some private, household workers. As seen early in Clinton's presidency, many household employers did not pay Social Security taxes for their employees.

With the growth of the contingent work force, more workers are being denied "entitlements." Contingent workers are also much more vulnerable to discrimination, harassment, and health and safety violations. As *Time* summed it up:

> Long-term commitments of all kinds are anathema to the modern corpora-
> tion. For the growing ranks of contingent workers, that means no more
> pensions, health insurance, or paid vacations. No more promises or pro-
> motions or costly training programs. No more lawsuits for wrongful termi-
> nation or other such hassles for the boss. . . Being a short-timer can mean
> doing hazardous work without essential training, or putting up with sexual
> and racial harassment. Placement officers report client requests for "blond
> bombshells" or people without accents. Says an agency counselor: "One
> client called and asked us not to send any Black people, and we didn't. We
> do whatever the clients want, whether it's right or not." [44]

Competing for Global Corporations

Workers will have to realize that they are now competing for jobs against
people who ride to work every day on bicycles, own only one pair of shabby
sandals, and are prepared [sic] to live with their families crammed into tiny
apartments.

—Robert Brusca, chief economist, Nikko Securities (New York)[45]

Like their colonial predecessors, global corporations see the world as
their farm, factory, mine, market, and playground.[46] The yearly sales of the
leading corporations dwarf the GNPs of most nations (Gross National Product
is a nation's total output of goods and services). The top *Fortune* 500 industrial corporation, General Motors, had sales of $134 billion in 1993, about
the GNP of Denmark and bigger than those of Saudi Arabia, South Africa,
Thailand, and Indonesia. The World Bank estimates that a third or more of
world trade consists of transfers within the 350 largest global corporations.
"By 1991 more than half of all U.S. exports and imports were transfers of
components and services within the same global corporation, most of them
flying the American flag"[47] (see table 12).

By the logic of the global corporation, the role of national and international government is to regulate the movement of labor, not capital. Non-
citizen immigrants may be treated as "aliens"—denied government assistance and deported— but not foreign corporations. By the logic of the global corporation, governments should subsidize the profits and socialize the
costs of business. By corporate logic, national bans on cancer-causing chemi-
cals, for example, may be prohibited internationally as unfair trade practices. By corporate logic, government should enforce corporate freedom,
not the rights of workers or consumers, through international "free trade"
agreements, finance and "development" agencies, as well as political, police, and military intervention.

Table 12
Countries with the Most Companies in the Fortune 500
World's Largest Industrial Corporations, 1993

	Number	Change Since 1992
United States	159	–2
Japan	135	+7
Britain	41	+1
Germany	32	no change
France	26	–4
South Korea	12	no change
Sweden	12	–2
Australia	10	+1
Switzerland	9	no change

Source: *Fortune*, July 25, 1994, p. 138.

Cities, states, and nations compete with each other in a no-win "race to the bottom" for corporate favor. There is no assurance subsidized corporations will stay. Many do not. According to a study by the Louisiana Coalition for Tax Justice: "To get a small handful of new jobs and corporations, Louisiana gave away $2.5 billion [between 1980 and 1989]. . . The taxpayer cost per full-time job created was $41,806. Tax breaks granted to six of the state's major polluters cost taxpayers more than $500,000 for each new permanent job created." [48]

As author Robert Goodman puts it, "This kind of public entrepreneuring . . . [has left] government in the role of competitor and business as welfare recipient. It is a process in which the public takes enormous financial risks, while business surveys the willing suitors and moves freely to where the public risk-taking is greatest." [49] This is how New Mexico beat California recently in a bid for Intel Corporation's new computer-chip factory:

New Mexico. . . could do what California couldn't: slash red tape, offer attractive tax breaks, and present a reformed, lower-cost workers' compensation system. But despite losing out to Rio Rancho, New Mexico, California still got something valuable out of its losing effort: a blunt lesson showing what must be done to compete more forcefully next time around. . .

The New Mexico package gave Intel $114 million worth of incentives: $57 million in property-tax abatements, $36 million in waived new-equipment sales taxes, $20 million in manufacturing tax credits, and $1 million in job-training funds. That amounts to $114,000 in concessions for each job Intel creates. . .

But complicating any potential change in California is a politically charged question: Should a state running an $8.6 billion budget deficit offer incentives to a company like Intel that doesn't need, but expects them?

Intel, after all, earned better than $1 billion last year on sales of $5.8 billion, mostly from its wildly popular microprocessors, the brains inside nearly 100 million personal computers. That makes Intel one of the most profitable companies in the world. . .

"We're going to build where Intel gets the best deal," said Intel's [Robert] Perlman. "California has to remember it doesn't do much good to have taxes on the books that it doesn't collect because companies don't build there." [50]

Free Trading On Cheap Labor

Gaining access to cheaper labor was the most important factor in U.S. companies' decisions to invest in [Caribbean] Basin assembly plants.
— U.S. General Accounting Office,
U.S. Support for Caribbean Basin Assembly Industries,
December 1993.

Corporate strategies maximize the ability of corporations to invest and *disinvest* rapidly, regardless of the impact on workers or communities— whether in Pennsylvania, Puerto Rico, Ireland, California, Mexico, Russia, or China. Corporations are aggressively automating and "downsizing" their work forces and shifting operations in a continual search for greater public subsidies and higher private profits, lower taxes, less regulation, and cheaper labor.

"Cheap labor" does not mean low-skill. Corporations are already switching to lower-paid, high-skilled industrial and service sector employees such as computer programmers and engineers. As *Business Week* put it in an article on the "push East" by European companies, "Western Europe's backyard has both Philippine-level industrial wages and well-trained engineers." [51] Bob Funk, president of the Oklahoma City-based Express Personnel Services, which staffed Moscow's first McDonald's, says Express has a roster of 65,000 Russian applicants, mostly college-educated, "who will work for 38 cents an hour." [52]

Software programming is increasingly "outsourced" to Third World countries where, in the words of *Computer Dealer News*, "the skills of highly educated computer professionals can be obtained at incredibly low cost. India and China, in particular, are being viewed as treasure troves of programming talent." More than 100 companies, including Hewlett-Packard and Motorola, have set up operations in India's high-tech center in Bangalore. According to the International Labor Organization, the typical programmer in India makes approximately $2,400 a year. [53] "Since the late 1970s, American computer companies have been coming to India to take advantage of well-trained but relatively low-paid computer engineers. At Motorola, for instance, a mid-level engineer makes $800 a month." [54]

In the words of a *Business Week* cover story on Mexico and NAFTA, Mexican workers are "smart, motivated, cheap." At this writing, U.S. minimum wage comes out to a mere $34 for an eight-hour day. In Mexico it was much worse, at $30 a week before the 1994 peso devaluation. NAFTA boosters pretend that wages will rise along with productivity, but between 1980 and 1993, the Mexican minimum wage fell 56 percent, adjusting for inflation, while factory productivity rose a reported 41 percent. A quarter of the business executives polled by the *Wall Street Journal* openly admitted they are likely to use NAFTA to bargain down wages and benefits in their U.S. plants by threatening to relocate in Mexico. [55] The recent peso devaluation and austerity program mean even lower living standards for Mexican workers.

Global corporations often operate in "free trade zones" (also called "export processing zones"). Repression is used to keep free trade zones free of labor unions as well as health and safety regulations. The typical free trade zone factory worker is a poorly paid young woman. Sexual harassment by male supervisors is common. So is exposure to toxic substances. [56]

The National Labor Committee in Support of Worker and Human Rights in Central America has exposed how U.S. tax dollars are used to promote runaway plants by supporting, among other things, ads like this one from 1990. The U.S. government backed the Salvadoran ruling families and military, their death squads and their political front men, to make sure El Salvador stayed a "best buy" for corporations.

Posing as the owners of New Age Textiles, National Labor Committee investigators were hosted in Honduras by the U.S.-supported Honduran Foundation for Investment and Development (FIDE). At various U.S.-supported free trade zones, they were told how labor organizing is prevented with computerized blacklists. One zone manager "explained that the blacklist includes all the names of people dismissed for whatever reason from any zone in the country. This way, New Age Textiles would be able to present a list of job applicants to the zone management and 'we check it out and will. . . tell you, okay, you have to get rid of this one or you have to get rid of that one.' " [57]

In a follow-up report, the National Labor Committee showed how the

Quality, Industriousness and Reliability Is What El Salvador Offers You!

Rosa Martinez produces apparel for U.S. markets on her sewing machine in El Salvador. <u>You</u> can hire her for 57-cents an hour*.

Rosa is more than just colorful. She and her co-workers are known for their industriousness, reliability and quick learning. They make El Salvador one of the best buys in the C.B.I. In addition, El Salvador has excellent road and sea transportation (including Central America's most modern airport) . . **and** there are **no** quotas.

Find out more about **sourcing** in El Salvador. Contact **FUSADES**, the private, non-profit and non-partisan organization promoting social and economic development in El Salvador. Miami telephone: **305/381-8940**.

*Does not include fringe benefits.

See us in Bobbin Show Booth 28/42

Circle #85 on Reader Service Card

Bobbin, August 1990 121

U.S. Commerce Department, the U.S. Agency for International Development (AID), and the World Bank lured corporations to the Caribbean with promises of tax giveaways, cheap labor, and no unions. The Commerce Department sent the following 1991 letter to over 1,000 U.S. businesses:

> The Informational Industries Mission to Barbados and Jamaica will allow a select dozen U.S. firms to evaluate and take advantage of prescreened business opportunities in the developing world's two leading offshore centers for information processing. . .
>
> Barbados and Jamaica offer a unique combination of educated, low-cost workers; highly developed telecommunications services; and geographic proximity; which together equal profitability and productivity for U.S. information companies.
>
> Over the past ten years many of your colleagues and competitors have expanded into the Caribbean, creating a growing pool of experienced workers and managers. . . With labor rates that range from just $1.00-$3.00 per hour, you can imagine the types of margins which these firms are enjoying.
>
> For the reasons cited, you owe it to your company to consider expanding in the Caribbean. This Mission offers the perfect opportunity, because it puts to work for you some 20 U.S. and Caribbean government and business officials.[58]

Candidates Bill Clinton and Al Gore blasted the Bush administration for promoting corporate flight. The Clinton administration's corporate stance is symbolized by the decision to officially de-link human rights from economic relations with China. U.S. officials boast of "commercial diplomacy" and "commercial engagement." As Commerce Secretary Ron Brown put it on an August 1994 trip to China, "We intend to compete in this market, and we intend to win."[59]

The Stride Rite Corporation, long renowned for its day care facilities and philanthropy, is a cofounder of Businesses for Social Responsibility. However, as the *Wall Street Journal* reports, over the last decade Stride Rite has "prospered partly by closing 15 factories, mostly in the Northeast and several in depressed areas, and moving most of its production to various low-cost Asian countries." There, "Stride Rite continues its quest for labor bargains. In recent years, it has switched from factories in South Korea as pay rose there to lower-wage Indonesia and China." A Stride Rite director says. "It has become sort of Holy Grail for us." In China, skilled workers "earn $100 to $150 a month, working 50 to 65 hours a week. Unskilled workers—packers and sorters—get $50 to $70 a month."[60]

Of course, Stride Rite is not alone in combining social rights and wrongs. The "socially-responsible" Esprit clothing company, for example, uses San Francisco garment contractors that pay below-minimum sweatshop wages with no overtime pay.[61]

Children are the cheapest laborers on the global assembly line and in the global plantation. Child labor is on the rise in the United States and around the world—along with adult unemployment. "Bangladesh, for example, has become one of the top ten apparel exporters to the United States by the widespread use of child labor. . . The NBC-TV program *Dateline* accused the Wal-Mart retail chain of contracting for the production of garments in a Bangladesh factory where over 60 percent of the 500 workers were children under the age of 13, working up to 20 hours a day and sleeping on the factory floor, earning as little as $7.50 a month." [62] Meanwhile, the family of the late Sam Walton, founder of Wal-Mart, has the world's greatest fortune, with a net worth of nearly $22 billion, according to *Forbes*.

In the United States, reported the General Accounting Office in 1992, the number of illegally employed minors, children under age 14, had nearly tripled since 1983. William Halperin, then associate director for surveillance at the National Institute for Occupational Safety and Health, called the findings "astounding," yet probably only "the tip of an iceberg." [63]

[With headquarters in Beaverton, Oregon] Nike is the number-one maker of sport shoes in the world. . .

Virtually 100 percent of Nike's shoe assembly is in Asia. In the last five years, the company has closed down twenty production sites in South Korea and Taiwan as wages have risen, and opened up thirty-five new ones in China, Indonesia, and Thailand, where wages are rock bottom. The company has a global payroll of over 8,000, virtually all in management, sales, promotion, and advertising. The actual production is in the hands of about 75,000 Asian contractors.

. . . Nikes made in Indonesia cost $5.60 to produce, and sell on the average in North America and Europe for $73 and as much as $135. The Indonesian girls [sic] who sew them can earn as little as fifteen cents an hour. (A 1991 survey of Nike-licensed plants, reported in *Indonesia Today*, put the average wage for an experienced female worker at $.82 a day.) Overtime is often mandatory, and after an eleven-hour day that begins at 7:30 A.M., the girls return to the company barracks at 9:15 P.M. to collapse into bed, having earned as much as $2.00 if they are lucky.

—Richard Barnet and John Cavanagh, *Global Dreams*.

Full of Unemployment

We never meant to quit our jobs. They quit on us.
—Former Rath Meatpacking employee from Waterloo, Iowa.[64]

There are 35 million people unemployed in OECD countries. Perhaps another 15 million have either given up looking for work or unwillingly accepted a part-time job. As many as a third of young workers in some OECD countries have no job.*
—Organization for Economic Cooperation and Development,
The OECD Jobs Study, 1994.

According to the International Labor Office, at the beginning of 1994 there were at least 120 million registered unemployed worldwide. Although this figure is by itself alarming, it does not include those who never registered as unemployed or those who stopped looking for a job because they regarded further search as futile. In addition, there were about 700 million workers that were underemployed, i.e., engaged in an economic activity that did not permit them to reach a minimum standard of living.
—UNCTAD, *World Investment Report 1994.*

While some workers have "jobs with no futures," others have "futures without jobs." The official U.S. unemployment rate averaged 4.5 percent in the 1950s, 4.7 percent in the 1960s, 6.2 percent in the 1970s, and 7.3 percent in the 1980s—not counting growing numbers of "discouraged" and other jobless and involuntary part-time workers, as discussed below.[65] The 1990s began with another official recession followed by a so-called "jobless recovery." That's like declaring recovery for a patient resuscitated into a coma.

The prevailing definition of "full employment" has gotten steadily less full of employment and more full of unemployment. The national "full employment" unemployment target of about 3 percent lasted from the mid-

---

* The OECD includes the United States, Canada, European Union countries, Japan, Australia, and New Zealand.

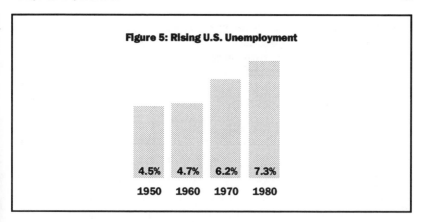

Figure 5: Rising U.S. Unemployment

4.5%	4.7%	6.2%	7.3%
1950	1960	1970	1980

1940s until the 1970s, when it moved to 4 percent under the Humphrey-Hawkins bill. Economic movers and shakers believe today's structural or "natural rate" of unemployment is 6 to 6.5 percent. Business does not want real full employment because workers would then be freer to reject jobs with poor working conditions and have more leverage to raise wages. Business leaders say they don't want the "wage inflation" of wages outpacing productivity but, as we have seen, wages are falling behind both productivity and price inflation.

The Federal Reserve has helped keep the supply of surplus labor high by raising interest rates to keep inflation extremely low—cheering the now famous bond market investors. Edward Herman, professor of finance at the Wharton School, University of Pennsylvania, says that "the more recent shift to an almost pathological fear of inflation reflects the growth in power of the financial community of brokers, bankers, and investors." He explains:

> In earlier years, before the rise of the global bond market and NRU [Natural Rate of Unemployment] theorizing, inflation was seen as a menace, but only in its extreme forms. Even conservative economists often argued that a gently rising price level was possibly ideal, as it would provide small entrepreneurial profit windfalls at the expense of coupon clippers (bond holders), would soften wage struggles by making it easier to raise money wages, and would serve as a general economic stimulus. The idea that inflation, once started, would necessarily get worse, was not a great concern, and is not supported by history. The historic U.S. inflations have never fit the NRU model of acceleration based on a policy of too rigorous efforts to reduce unemployment; they have been rooted in excess demand and speculation resulting from war spending, the release of pent-up war demand, and accumulated high liquidity (1945-48), or fear of war and its

effects (Korea, 1950-52). The inflationary spurt in the late 1960s and 1970s was linked to Vietnam war deficits and the oil cartel's price increases of 1973 and 1979. Only external shocks have driven inflation levels over 5 percent in modern U.S. experience.[66]

The Federal Reserve continues its war on inflation, which is low, at the expense of employment.

Corporations call layoffs "downsizing." Information technology is making middle managers expendable, along with clerical and assembly workers. Between 1979 and 1992, the total worldwide employment of the *Fortune* 500 dropped from 16.2 million to 11.8 million.[67] In 1993, the *Fortune* 500 had profits of $62.6 billion. *Fortune* says what makes that year's profits "even more impressive is that sales growth in 1993 was virtually stagnant. So by all means, join in with Maureen Allyn, chief economist of Scudder Stevens & Clark, who declares, 'Hats off to America's industrial heartland.' "

Fortune adds, "Employees, though, might well voice a few loud gripes. . . Total employment among the 500 fell for the ninth straight year [to 11.5 million]. . . while median employment dropped 5.3 percent, to 10,136. Often the jobs that remained were far less lucrative. Caterpillar, for example, forced the United Auto Workers to accept a two-tier wage system. . . Scudder's Maureen Allyn: 'U.S. industry needed to get lean and mean, but we probably went overboard.' "[68]

"Hot Damn! They Did It Again," *Business Week* declared as profits for the 900 U.S. companies in their Corporate Scoreboard matched "the staggering 45 percent profit gain of the second quarter" of 1994 by jumping 45 percent in the third quarter, as corporate sales rose 10 percent. How did earnings rise three times faster than sales? Here's what *Business Week* says:

> What's making companies so profitable? It's a simple matter of productivity and its brake on labor costs. . . Unit labor costs, the wages and benefits that go into producing a good or service, are growing by less than 1 percent—a pace not seen since the early 1960s. Among manufacturers, unit labor costs fell 2.7 percent in the third quarter [of 1994]. By contrast, the price of goods and services climbed 2.8 percent in the same period.
>
> Restructuring has also helped pump up [profit] margins. By slashing payrolls, investing in technology, or simply overhauling assembly lines, companies are making more efficient use of fewer workers. . .
>
> The huge pool of labor has a lot to do with the prevailing wage restraint. True, the jobless rate has fallen to 5.9 percent, from 7.3 percent a year ago.

But that's only part of the story. The unemployment statistics don't count the roughly 4 million part-time workers who are eager for full-time jobs. In addition, the explosive increase in the number of temporary workers gives few employees much leverage in negotiating pay raises.[69]

Corporations are betting that the rising disposable incomes of "winners" in the global economy will compensate for falling incomes among disposable workers. It's a shortsighted bet. It's more likely that all this job-eliminating downsizing will be equivalent to farmers selling their seed corn. Short-term profit for long-term disaster. Some call it "corporate anorexia."

The evidence about the impact of downsizing on company performance to date is mixed. According to the 1994 American Management Association survey—whose respondents are mostly major companies, nearly half of them in manufacturing—"51 percent of companies reporting workforce reductions since January 1989 reported an increase in operating profits after the cuts; 20 percent said operating profits declined. . . Productivity gains have been even more elusive. Among all firms reporting reductions, only a third said productivity increased; nearly as many (30 percent) said it had declined. . . The surest aftereffect of downsizing is a negative impact on employee morale, which suffered in 86 percent of all firms reporting cuts any time since January 1989." According to the survey, "workforce reductions begin to show more positive effects some three years after the most recent round of cuts—although time does little to heal the surest effect of downsizing, a negative impact on employee morale."[70]

In *Business Week*'s words, "This is the bleak underside of the new workplace: For every empowered employee, there's at least another cowering in his office, putting in longer hours to keep up with a job that used to keep two people busy. For every highly skilled worker moving up the ladder, there's another, marginalized, struggling to make ends meet."[71]

Instead of hiring new employees, many companies are automating and overworking their remaining employees. In the face of mass unemployment during the Great Depression, the American Federation of Labor (AFL) called for a 30-hour week in 1932. In 1933, the U.S. Senate passed a bill mandating a 30-hour week for all businesses engaged in interstate and foreign commerce. A survey of business executives by the Industrial Conference Board found that more than half had reduced the number of hours worked to save jobs and promote consumer spending. The Kellogg Com-

pany had switched to a 6-hour day in 1930. As Harvard economist Juliet
Schor tells it, "They were searching for a strategy to cope with the unemployment of the Depression. To their surprise, they found that workers were
more productive, on the order of 3 percent to 4 percent. . . According to W.
K. Kellogg, 'the efficiency and morale of our employees is [sic] so increased, the accident and insurance rates are so improved, and the unit cost
of production is so lowered, that we can afford to pay as much for six hours
as we formerly paid for eight.' " Unfortunately, President Roosevelt—who
later came to regret it—joined with business leaders to kill the 30-hour
legislation.[72]

According to the American Management Association survey, "policies
intended to 'share the pain' and lessen job loss, by reducing pay or hours or
spreading the work, are generally in decline. Rather than *share* work to save
jobs, many companies do the opposite, *expanding* the work day for those
still employed. Half of the firms that have downsized since 1988 say they
have extended working hours and/or overtime as an alternative to new hiring."[73]

Compared to the late 1960s, "the average worker is working about an
extra month of work per year," writes Harvard economist Juliet Schor. "Factory overtime has now reached its highest recorded level. . . In the automobile industry, where tens of thousands of workers have been laid off, daily
overtime has become standard. In the Detroit area the average workweek is
47.5. . . The UAW estimates that 59,000 automobile jobs would be created
if the plants were on a 40-hour week."[74] In May 1994, the average U.S.
worker at auto and supplier plants logged a record 7.9 hours a week of
overtime.

In Fall 1994, more than 11,000 auto workers went on a three-day strike
at Buick City in Flint, Michigan, with the demand that General Motors hire
more workers, rather than continue its practice of forced overtime, which
was robbing the workers of health, leisure, and time for family and other
responsibilities. Workers "were averaging 10 hours a day on the job, routinely worked one weekend day, and, at times, were forced to put in seven
days a week on the factory floor."[75] That strike was settled when GM agreed
to hire more workers, but more strikes against forced overtime and layoff-
induced understaffing have followed.

Corporations are demanding that employees cooperate in corporate restructuring—through worker-management teams, quality circles, and so on—without sharing in the benefits of resulting increased productivity and profit. As *Business Week* puts it, "We increasingly demand that our workers take on responsibility and risk, yet their pay is falling. Will $8-an-hour machinists do high-performance work?" They quote MIT professor Paul Osterman: "You can't expect workers to keep contributing their ideas when they don't get rewarded for them." [76]

The main supposed inducement for worker cooperation is continued employment at a time of high unemployment, but often even that is not the case, as illustrated by Romie Manan's testimony to the Commission on the Future of Worker-Management Relations about his experience at National Semiconductor's plant in Santa Clara:

> Manan explained how National had told workers that they had to team up with management in order to beat Japanese competition. Fearing for their jobs, he said, workers agreed. "Increasing the company's profitability, they said, would increase our job security," Manan testified. "That was the purpose of the teams—to make us more efficient and productive... We became more efficient... Then the company took the ideas contributed by the experienced workforce in Santa Clara... and used them to organize new fabs [fabrication lines] with inexperienced workers in Arlington, Texas, where wages are much lower. Then the experienced workers lost their jobs." [77]

Measuring Unemployment

The U.S. government downsizes the unemployment rate, but not the reality, much as it does poverty. There's a large gap between the number of people wanting jobs and the number included in the unemployment rate. The official rate doesn't include would-be workers who have searched for work in the past year, or even the last five weeks—but not in the past *four* weeks. The official rate leaves out people defined as "discouraged workers," people with child care problems, and millions of others without jobs. It doesn't include involuntary part-timers (see table 13).

Business Week observes: "Increasingly the labor market is filled with surplus workers who are not being counted as unemployed. The rate of labor force participation—those working or looking for work—has dropped sharply for men since 1989. Estimated conservatively, some 1.1 million prime-age male workers are out of the labor force compared with five years ago. . . And there are at least 500,000 more workers with some college who have jobs but are underemployed compared to five years ago." [78]

The Labor Department acknowledged in late 1993 that the government had been substantially underestimating unemployment among women. Blatant sexism biased the unemployment surveying. As more women worked outside the home, government interviewers continued to begin their survey this way: When men responded the interviewer typically asked, "What were you doing most of last week, working or something else?" Women were typically asked whether they were "keeping house or something else." If they answered keeping house, the interviewer didn't bother to find out if they were laid off or looking for work; so even if they were, the government counted them as homemakers, not unemployed members of the work force When the government refigured the overall official unemployment rate fo the 12 months through August 1993 it was 7.6 percent, not 7.1 percent.[7] Women's unemployment rate would be even higher if the government in cluded "discouraged workers" and people not currently looking for wor because of child care problems, for example.

Alternative unemployment and underemployment measures, such as th

Urban League's "Hidden Unemployment Index," have typically adjusted the official rate by adding in "discouraged workers" and involuntary part-timers—two categories that the Labor Department made more restrictive beginning in 1994, resulting in lower official numbers. David Dembo and Ward Morehouse advocate an alternative "jobless rate," which reflects the larger pool of jobless workers (including "discouraged") and adjusts for involuntary part-time employment using a full-time equivalence formula. Their 1993 jobless rate is 13.8 percent. Dembo and Morehouse observe:

> The Jobless Rate—about twice the official Unemployment Rate—rises and falls with the official rate. However, as more people are forced to work part-time, and as increasing numbers have dropped out of the official labor force altogether, the Jobless Rate tends to diverge even more from the official rate. During cyclical downturns (recessions). . . the Jobless Rate increases more than does the Unemployment Rate as record numbers of Americans give up looking for work and more and more people work part-time for economic reasons. . . With each succeeding recovery period, the Jobless Rate has fallen less and less.[80]

Official Black unemployment is more than double the White rate; the Latino rate is almost double the White rate (see tables 13 and 14). "Even at the peak of the last business cycle in 1989, the 11.4 percent unemployment among Black workers was higher than the average unemployment reached in any post-war *recession*." (Italics in original.) The official Black rate averaged 14.1 percent between 1976 and 1993.[81] As the official unemployment rates for Black and White workers dropped in 1994, diverging even further from the real Jobless Rates, the Federal Reserve stepped up its efforts to slow down the economy.

People with disabilities are especially hard hit in a high-unemployment economy. According to Patricia Kirkpatrick, who is writing a report on the status of people with disabilities, "Statistics in this area are not current or complete, but they indicate that as many as 66 percent of all working-age Americans with disabilities [and over 77 percent of working-age Blacks with disabilities] are unemployed. The major causes have to do with exclusionary practices and attitudes of employers, inaccessible work environments, and inadequate levels of education."[82] Educational attainment may also reflect discrimination. Looking at persons 21 to 64 years old, the Census Bureau report, *Americans With Disabilities: 1991-92*, found that 80.5 percent of those with no disability were employed and only 52 percent of those with a disability were employed. The respective figures for men are 88.8 percent and 59.1 percent; for women, 72.6 percent and 45.2 percent. The employment rate is much lower for those categorized as having a "severe disability," defined, for example, as using a wheelchair, or being a long-term user of canes or crutches, or having developmental disabilities. Only 23.2 percent of persons 21 to 64 years old with a severe disability were employed. Other government reports measure by "work disability" status. But as *Americans With Disabilities* explains, "the work disability question implies that the only factor affecting the ability to work is the condition of the person. This is clearly not the case. Under one set of environmental factors, a given condition may hinder or prevent work, but if physical and/or social barriers are removed, the same condition may have no effect on the ability to work."[83]

To make matters worse for all the unemployed, unemployment insurance is not ensuring. Less than half of all officially unemployed workers receive any unemployment benefits. And unemployment benefits have fallen behind inflation. Low-wage workers and contingent workers—disproportionately women and people of color—are less likely than others to qualify for unemployment benefits (they may not meet work time or earnings requirements). When they do qualify, their temporary payments are only a fraction of their meager wages. The average unemployment benefit is only 37 percent of the average wage.[84] (And unemployment compensation has been taxed since 1978.) Eligibility varies by state and benefits typically last only a maximum of 26 weeks, whether or not you've found a job.

"Studies in several states have found that a substantial proportion of new AFDC (Aid to Families with Dependent Children) families are headed by individuals who have recently lost their jobs," reports the Center on Budget and Policy Priorities. "For unemployed people who do not have children, little or no cash assistance may be available if they fail to receive unemployment benefits."[85] In other words, there is no "safety net" for many people thrown out of work.

Table 13
A Closer Look at Unemployment and Underemployment, 1994

Government Definitions

"People are classified as *employed* if they did any work at all as paid employees during the [survey] reference week; worked in their own business, profession, or on their own farm; or worked without pay at least 15 hours in a family business or farm. People are also counted as employed if they were temporarily absent from their jobs because of illness, bad weather, vacation, labor-management disputes, or personal reasons," whether or not they were paid by their employers for time off.

"People are classified as *unemployed* if they meet all of the following criteria: They had no employment during the reference week; they were available for work at that time; and they made specific efforts to find employment sometime during the 4-week period ending with the reference week. Persons [temporarily] laid off from a job and expecting recall need not be looking for work to be counted as unemployed."

Official Unemployment Rates, Second Quarter 1994 *seasonally adjusted*

All Workers	White	Black	Latino	Men	Women	Teenagers
6.2	5.4	11.5	10.2	6.2	6.1	18.4

Joblessness and Involuntary Part-time Work, May 1994 Snapshot

	Total	Men	Women
Official Unemployed*	7.7 million	4.1 million	3.6 million
Not Included in Unemployment Rate			
Persons who currently want a job†	5.9 million	2.3 million	3.6 million
Searched for work & available	1.9 million	870 thousand	988 thousand
to work now (persons who have searched for work during prior 12 months and available to take a job during the reference week)			
Reason not currently looking			
Discouragement over job	521 thousand	314 thousand	207 thousand
prospects‡ (includes thinks no work available, could not find work, lacks schooling or training, employer thinks too young or old, and other types of discrimination)			
Reasons other than	1.3 million	556 thousand	781 thousand
discouragement (includes those who did not actively look for work in the prior 4 weeks for such reasons as child-care and transportation problems, as well as a small number for which reason not determined)			
Involuntary Part-time Workers*			
Part-time for Economic Reasons	4.3 million		

*Seasonally adjusted

†Not seasonally adjusted because of available data.

‡The categories for discouraged workers and for those working part time for economic reasons were narrowed significantly beginning in 1994, leading to a large reduction in the numbers of people counted. Discouraged workers were excluded from the unemployment rate in 1 9 6 7 .

Sources: U.S. Department of Labor, Bureau of Labor Statistics, "The Employment Situation: September 1994," October 7, 1994; *Employment and Earnings*, Third Quarter 1994 (October 1994).

"Technological Unemployment"

Today, the power of a personal-computer microchip doubles every 18 months.
                                            —*Business Week*, October 17, 1994.[86]

As bad as unemployment and underemployment are now, the situation is going to get much worse. Jeremy Rifkin, whose new book is called *The End of Work*, predicts that within a few decades hundreds of millions of people working globally in manufacturing, services, and agriculture could be displaced though automation, artificial intelligence, and biotechnology. "We are fast moving into a world where there will be factories without workers and agricultural production without farms or farmers," warns Rifkin.[87]

In the past, farmers and farmworkers displaced by the mechanization of agriculture were absorbed in large numbers by manufacturing. Many workers displaced by the earlier wave of manufacturing automation were absorbed by the service sector. There is no new industry capable of absorbing the millions of workers being displaced by automation and reengineering in the contemporary era of "thinking machines." Biotechnology, for example, is a low-employment industry. "The high-technology revolution is not normally associated with farming," writes Rifkin, but "technological changes in the production of food are leading to a world without farmers, with untold consequences for the 2.4 billion [people worldwide] who rely on the land for their survival."[88]

Between 1979 and 1992, manufacturing output rose 13 percent, while the workforce declined by 15 percent.[89] The Bureau of Labor Statistics predicts that between 1990 and 2005, "the value of goods manufactured in the United States will climb 41 percent. But the number of people employed to make those goods will fall 3 percent."[90]

As just-in-time production is shaking up the manufacturing sector, so too, "just-in-time retailing" will shake up that large part of the service sector. As *Forbes* puts it, "More Americans are shopping by computer, television, or telephone, buying what they want quickly and efficiently. And therein lies a very serious threat to the country's traditional retail industry and to the 19 million people it employs."[91] A shrinking number of workers and managers will be needed to sell discount goods at discount wages.

Today, U.S. and other corporations are shifting computer programming to countries like China and India. "Skeptics wonder whether offshore programmers will be needed at all in the years to come. For an increasingly large percentage of applications that aren't complex, most of the code may soon be generated by CASE (computer-aided software engineering) tools."[92]

In 1963, a committee of prominent scientists, economists, and academics, such as J. Robert Oppenheimer, Robert Theobald, and W. H. Ferry, called attention to *The Triple Revolution*: the Cybernation Revolution, the Weaponry Revolution, and the Human Rights Revolution. They warned: "A new era of production has begun. Its principles of organization are as different as those of the industrial era were different from those of the agricultural era. The cybernation revolution has been brought about by the combination of the computer and the automated self-regulating machine. This results in a system of almost unlimited productive capacity which requires progressively less human labor." As Rifkin points out, "The Committee acknowledged that 'The Negroes are the hardest hit of the many groups being exiled from the economy by cybernation,' but predicted that, in time, the new computer revolution would take over more and more of the productive tasks in the economy, leaving millions of workers jobless. The Committee urged the President and Congress to consider guaranteeing every citizen 'an adequate income as a matter of right.' "

President Johnson established a National Commission on Guaranteed Incomes in 1967. In supporting a guaranteed annual income, the Commission's report stated, "Unemployment or underemployment among the poor are often due to forces that cannot be controlled by the poor themselves. For many of the poor, the desire to work is strong but the opportunities are not. . . Even if the existing welfare and related programs are improved, they are incapable of assuring that all Americans receive an adequate income."[94] President Nixon's proposal for a small guaranteed annual income through the 1969 Family Assistance Plan satisfied no one.

Today, terms like cyberspace and virtual reality have become commonplace, and so have high unemployment and falling incomes. But proposals for a "guaranteed annual income" and a 30-hour week to "share the work" have not returned to the fore of public debate, much less been embraced by the U.S. government.

Hiding Bad Economics Behind Scapegoats

---

impoverish: 1 to make poor; 2 to deprive of strength, resources, etc.

poor: 1 having little or no means of support; needy 2 lacking in some quality; specif., a) inadequate b) inferior or worthless c) contemptible 3 worthy of pity; unfortunate

—Webster's New World Dictionary

"Since 1973," reports the Children's Defense Fund, "most of the fastest increases in poverty rates occurred among young White families with children, those headed by married couples, and those headed by high school graduates. For all three groups, *poverty rates more than doubled in a single generation*, reaching levels that most Americans commonly assume afflict only minority and single-parent families."[95] The poverty rates for children in young families headed by college graduates also more than doubled (see table 8).

The American Dream—always an impossible dream for many—is dying a slow death, and many are swallowing the snake oil of scapegoating. Scapegoating labels like "underclass," and myths like the "culture of poverty," make it easier to impoverish and disenfranchise lower income people. They also make it easier to impoverish and disenfranchise those who think of "the poor" as the "Other America," Them and not Us.

Setting the poverty line too low makes the Them versus Us distinction easier. The more people there are who officially are considered not poor, the easier it is to blame poverty on personal failings rather than systemic failings. Schwarz and Volgy explain that, in 1980, when official unemployment was over 7 percent, "in the public's mind, the foremost causes of poverty were that the poor weren't thrifty, that they did not put in the needed effort, and that they lacked ability or talent. Popular majorities did not consider any other factor to be a very important cause of poverty—not low wages, or a scarcity of jobs, or discrimination, or even sickness." [96]

"The poor are less obviously deserving today than they used to be," wrote an editor of the *Washington Monthly* in 1993. "Steinbeck's Joads [in *The Grapes of Wrath*] weren't criminals or drug addicts. . . Victims of the Depression or the sharecroppers who flooded the North after World War II could justifiably be portrayed as victims of upheaval." [98] "The old issues were economic and structural," asserts conservative political scientist Lawrence Mead. "The new ones are social and personal." In reality, as *The State of Working America* observes looking at the 1979 to 1992 period, "the major forces driving the increase in poverty rates were nondemographic factors, primarily wages and benefits." In addition, the system of government taxation and income support was less effective in reducing poverty. [98] Scapegoaters don't let reality get in their way.

A nationwide 1990 survey by the National Opinion Research Center at the University of Chicago—in which most respondents were White—found an abundance of racist stereotypes: 78 percent of the non-Black respondents said Blacks are more likely than Whites to "prefer to live off welfare" and less likely to "prefer to be self-supporting." In addition, 62 percent said Blacks are more likely to be lazy; 56 percent said Blacks are violence-prone; and 53 percent said Blacks are less intelligent. Among non-Latino respondents, 74 percent said Hispanics are more likely to prefer to live off welfare; 56 percent said they are more lazy; 50 percent thought them more violence-prone; and 55 percent said Hispanics are less intelligent. [99] Remember that at the time of this survey, the kind of racist pseudo-scientific views of intelligence promoted in *The Bell Curve* had not yet returned to center stage.

Stereotypes can influence perception of even unambiguous events. In one study, "subjects were shown pictures of a White man holding a razor during an argument with a Black man. When the pictures were described to others, the White subjects recalled the Black man as wielding the razor!" [100]

Stereotypes reinforce the supposed behavioral explanations of persistent poverty which provide cover for economies that persistently impoverish. Boston's Irish immigrants, for example, were portrayed as having a culture of poverty and violence a century before Oscar Lewis famously applied the term "culture of poverty" to Mexicans, Puerto Ricans, and African Americans. The "famine Irish" were economically exploited and socially stereotyped as immoral, drunkards, and criminals—hence the term "Paddy wagon" for police wagon. Alcoholism was once recorded in the Massachusetts registry as a cause of death for Irish immigrants, not for Protestant Anglo-Saxons. In the late nineteenth and early twentieth centuries, Italians, Greeks, Russian Jews, and other immigrants were also "labeled as 'dangerous and undesirable elements' " and "inferior." [101] As White immigrants, and especially their children, were assimilated, racism against African Americans—who, unlike Whites, were systematically, violently enslaved and segregated—remained virulent.

The U.S. Constitution once defined Black slaves as worth three-fifths of a human being. Today, Black per capita income is three-fifths that of Whites. That's an economic measure of racism. The Latino-White ratio is even worse. [102]

Scapegoating fuels fear and fear fuels scapegoating. California's 1994 "Save Our State (SOS)" Proposition 187 denies public education, non-emergency medical care, and social services to undocumented immigrants and requires teachers, doctors, social service providers, and police to report suspected illegal immigrants to immigration and other authorities. Though at this writing it is not technically in force while its constitutionality is contested in the courts, Proposition 187 is already taking a toll. It is no accident that growing anti-immigrant sentiment and action target Latinos and other immigrants of color rather than Canadian, Italian, Irish, Polish, and other White immigrants, documented and undocumented. Immigrants are blamed for sapping California's economy and the nation's. Never mind that the economy depends in part on immigrant labor and recent studies confirm that immigrants actually create more jobs than they fill and pay significantly more in taxes than the cost of the public services they receive. [103]

Blaming Women for Illegitimate Economics

Women are scapegoated as producers and reproducers of poverty. His-
torically, "women have been viewed as the breeders of poverty, criminality,
and other social problems," observes Mimi Abramovitz, professor of Social
Policy at the Hunter College School of Social Work. "From the 'tenement
classes' of the mid-1800s and the 'dangerous classes' of the 1880s, to Social Darwinism and eugenics, to Freudian theories of motherhood, to
Moynihan's 'Black matriarchy' and today's 'underclass,' society blames
women for the failed policies of business and the state." [104]

In *The Negro Family*, Daniel Patrick Moynihan, then a Labor Department official and now a U.S. senator, embellished sociologist E. Franklin
Frazier's thesis of the Black matriarch in whom "neither economic necessity nor tradition had instilled the spirit of subordination to masculine au-
thority." Moynihan claimed in his 1965 report that matriarchal families are
at the core of a Black "tangle of pathology"—and this, not racism, was the
"fundamental source of the weakness of the Negro Community." The civil
rights movement was then struggling to dismantle U.S. apartheid
Moynihan's thesis was the antithesis to the Black liberation movement
feminism, and the welfare rights movement. The White House released the
report shortly after the Watts riots.

Today, liberals and conservatives alike accuse single mothers, especially
Black single mothers, of putting their children and all society at risk.[105]
Imagine labeling married-couple families as pathological breeding grounds
of patriarchal domestic violence, or suggesting that women should never
marry, because they are more likely to be beaten and killed by a spouse than
a stranger.[106] Liberals have joined with Dan Quayle and company in their
attack on real-life Murphy Browns and her less privileged sisters. Secretary
of Health and Human Services Donna Shalala, former chair of the Children's
Defense Fund, told *Newsweek*, "I don't like to put this in moral terms, but
I do believe that having children out of wedlock is just wrong." She told the
House Ways and Means Committee, "I don't think anyone in public life

today ought to condone children born out of wedlock. . . even if the family is financially able." [107] President Clinton told the National Baptist Convention in September 1994, "I know not everybody is going to be in a stable, traditional family like you see in one of those 1950 sitcoms, but we'd be better off if more people were." He preached, "You shouldn't have a baby when you're not married. You just have to stop it." The president should read Stephanie Coontz's book, *The Way We Never Were: American Families and the Nostalgia Trap*, among other things.

The awful labeling of children as "illegitimate" has again been legitimized. Besides meaning born out of wedlock, illegitimate also means illegal, contrary to rules and logic, misbegotten, not genuine, wrong—to be, a bastard. Single mothers and their children, especially Black women and children, have become prime scapegoats for illegitimate economics. In the past, "the bodies of Black women became political terrain on which some proponents of White [and male] supremacy mounted their campaigns," observes Ricki Solinger in her historical study of single motherhood and race, and "the Black illegitimate baby became the child White politicians and taxpayers loved to hate." [108] So it goes today. Never mind that impoverished women don't create poverty any more than slaves created slavery.

Stigma is accompanied by negative expectations and prejudicial treatment. In a study cited by Stephanie Coontz, "teachers shown a videotape of a child engaging in a variety of actions consistently rate the child much more negatively on a wide range of dimensions when they are told that he or she comes from a divorced family, than when they believe the child to come from an intact home." [109]

Contrary to stereotype, single mother families increased at a higher rate in the 1970s than in the 1980s or 1990s. This was true for those headed by never-married women as well as divorced women. True for Blacks as well as Whites. And true even though a significant portion of the increase since 1980 is due to changes in Census Bureau survey procedures. [110] Moreover, the typical women behind the rise in never-married mothers in the 1980s, says the U.S. General Accounting Office, "differed from the stereotype: They were not unemployed teenaged dropouts, but rather working women aged 25 to 44 who had completed high school." Also contrary to image, the *proportion* of Black children born to unmarried mothers (most of them not teenagers) is growing because the birth rates of *married* Black women have fallen so dramatically.[111] It's also important to understand that the term "single-parent" does not necessarily mean that the family does not have two parents living together; it may mean two parents who are not legally married. "It has become increasingly likely that a child born to an unmarried mother is not actually born into a single-parent family." There has been a large rise in the number of families composed of unmarried couples—heterosexual and homosexual—with children.[112]

The proportion of households headed by women has been rising in all regions of the world. Women are reported to be the sole breadwinners in one-fourth to one-third of the world's families. "Studies in many nations show that it is more often women's income that meets the family's basic needs, such as food, clothing, health care, and education."[113] In the words of a congressional report, "Almost all major industrialized countries have experienced large increases in the number of births to unmarried women." As of 1991, the number of births to unmarried women as a percentage of all live births was 48 percent in Sweden, 47 percent in Denmark, 30 percent in the United Kingdom, 30 percent in France (1990), 30 percent in the United States, 29 percent in Canada, and 15 percent in Germany.[114] These other countries do not have U.S. proportions of poverty.

It shouldn't be surprising that in the United States, Black and Latino families—whether one-parent or two-parent families—have higher poverty rates than White families, since the wages and job opportunities of people of color reflect educational and employment discrimination. It shouldn't be surprising that single-parent families have high rates of poverty since, with the fall in real wages, two or more incomes are increasingly needed to keep families out of poverty. Since single mothers of color experience both race and gender discrimination, their families are the most impoverished. Nationally, 46 percent of all female-headed families with children under 18 were below the official 1993 poverty line, as were 23 percent of male-headed families with children (no wives present). In other words, single father families have very high rates of poverty, but single mother families have even higher rates. The official 1993 poverty rates were 40 percent for White single mothers, 20 percent for White single fathers; 58 percent for Black single mothers, 32 percent for Black fathers; 61 percent for Latina single mothers and 28 percent for Latino single fathers.[115]

Instead of rooting out discrimination, encouraging adequate wages, promoting full and flexible employment, and implementing the kind of child care and other family supports common in numerous countries, many U.S. policy makers are busily blaming women for their disproportionate poverty. For women, "wage discrimination is worse in the United States than in any other major developed country except Japan." [116]

The fact that many female-headed households are poorer because women are generally paid less than men is taken as a given in much poverty policy discussion, as if pay equity were a pipe dream not even worth mentioning. A 1977 government study found that if working women were paid what similarly qualified men earn, the number of poor families would decrease by half. [117] A 1991 government study found that "many single mothers will remain near or below the poverty line even if they work at full-time jobs. Problems they are likely to face include low earnings; vulnerability to layoffs and other work interruptions; lack of important fringe benefits such as paid sick leave and health insurance; and relatively high expenses for child care." [118]

Most mothers work outside the home as well as inside. But you wouldn't know that by looking at school hours, the scarcity of after-school programs, and affordable day care. More than half of all women with children under age 6, and three-fourths of women with children ages 6 to 17, are in the paid work force. By 1993, only 10 percent of all families, and only 21 percent of families with children under 18, fit the stereotype of a 1950s family with a breadwinner father and a homemaker mother who cares for the children and does not work outside the home. [119]

Despite the obvious need, subsidized child care is scarce. The federal tax deduction for child care expenses is capped at an absurdly low amount, and then reduced further, depending on income, resulting in an average taxpayer credit projected at $435 for 1994—for a projected total credit of $2.7 billion. By contrast, mortgage interest is fully deductible on acquisition debt of up to $1 million for first and second homes. The 1993 tax revenue loss for the mortgage interest deduction, disproportionately benefiting higher-income families, was $44 billion. [120] When it comes to child care, women are hit at both ends, paying large sums for care while earning so little as child care teachers that many can't even afford to enroll their own children in the centers where they work. Nationally, child care teaching staff, nearly all women, had average earnings of only $9,363 in 1988, while sanitation workers earned $19,163 and workers in cigarette factories earned $30,590. People who take care of animals in zoos make on average $2,500 more a year than child care teachers.[121]

In the words of a comprehensive study commissioned by the Boston Foundation, after food, housing, and taxes, child care is the biggest expense for working parents of all incomes. "For moderate-income families, child care costs can swamp dreams of going back to school, home ownership, or savings for college. For the working poor and for low-income families, subsidized child care can be the key to staying off welfare, to getting an education, a better job, and housing." [122]

The writers and scholars and politicians who wax most rhapsodic about the need to replace welfare with work make their harsh judgments from the comfortable and supportive environs of offices and libraries and think tanks. If they need to go to the bathroom midsentence, there is no one timing their absence. If they take longer than a half-hour for lunch, there is no one waiting to dock their pay. If their baby-sitter gets sick, there is no risk of someone having taken their place at work by the next morning. Yet these are conditions that low-wage women routinely face, which inevitably lead to the cyclical nature of their welfare histories.

—Rosemary L. Bray, *New York Times Magazine*, November 8, 1992.

Reducing Welfare Instead of Poverty

Racist and sexist scapegoating have come together most viciously in the rollback of welfare. The demonization of the welfare mother, writes Rosemary Bray, reinforces the patriarchal notion "that women and children without a man are fundamentally damaged goods" and allows "for denial about the depth and intransigence of racism."[123] In the name of reform, politicians have substituted fighting welfare for fighting poverty. Myths crowd out realities.

In 1992 (the latest year of full data), there were 13.6 million AFDC recipients, including 9.2 million children. AFDC has not expanded at the rising pace of people in poverty, especially children. The number of AFDC child recipients, as a percent of children in poverty, has fallen from 81 percent in 1973, to 63 percent in 1992. About 39 percent of families receiving AFDC are White, 37 percent are Black (a lower percentage than 1973), 18 percent are Latino, 3 percent are Asian, and 1 percent are Native American. There are disproportionately more people of color on welfare because disproportionately more people of color are poor, unemployed and underemployed, and they have disproportionately less access to other government income support programs such as unemployment and workers' compensation. The official 1992 unemployment rate for women maintaining families was 7.8 percent for Whites and 14.7 percent for Blacks.[124] The real jobless and underemployment rates are much higher.

Scapegoaters don't care if women turn to AFDC after fleeing abusive husbands or after losing their jobs. Some women turn to AFDC to find health care. One study estimated that providing health insurance to all employed single mothers would reduce the AFDC caseload by about 10 percent. Many countries require paid maternity leave. The United States does not. An Ohio study found that a woman on pregnancy leave is ten times more likely to lose her job than one on medical leave for other reasons.[125] The Family and Medical Leave Act, finally enacted in 1993 with much struggle and fanfare, stipulates only unpaid leave, and excludes many workers. In Massachusetts, in the year following the Family Leave Act's passage, "few area employees have used the law, saying unpaid time off is a luxury they cannot afford." [126]

AFDC benefits have been cut repeatedly as if, once you have too little money, it doesn't matter how little you have. Between 1970 and 1994, the median state's maximum monthly benefit for a family of three was cut nearly in half (47 percent), adjusting for inflation, and the cutting continues. When food stamps are added to AFDC, the combined median benefit is still only 72 percent of the official poverty line. [127] (13 percent of families on AFDC don't receive food stamps.) Contrary to common belief, fewer than one out of four families receiving AFDC live in public housing or receive any rent subsidies. In 40 of 44 metro areas surveyed nationally, the cost of a modest two-bedroom apartment, according to HUD's Fair Market Rent level, is greater than the *entire* AFDC benefit for a family of three with no other income; in 28 metro areas, a one-bedroom apartment would cost more than the entire AFDC benefit for a family of three. [128]

A government report assessing poverty trends between 1980 and 1988, "found that the primary reason for the apparent poverty rate increase among women heading single-parent families living alone is the decrease in transfer payments, particularly reductions in means-tested assistance and social insurance. The poverty rate increase occurred despite the fact that these women were working more and earning more." According to a congressional report, "in 1979 approximately 30 percent of individuals in single-parent families were removed from poverty as the result of means-tested transfers, food, and housing benefits, and Federal tax policy. By 1990, this had declined to 20 percent." Meanwhile, "the percentage of elderly individuals removed from poverty due to social insurance programs increased from 68 percent to 73 percent from 1979 to 1990." [129]

Welfare budget-cutters pretend that AFDC is a major drain on public money when, in fact, it is not. AFDC accounted for about 1 percent of federal outlays in 1994 and states spent 2 percent of their revenues on AFDC. The gap between image and reality is vast. For example, a poll of 1994 voters found that one out of five believed that welfare was *the largest federal government expense*, larger even than defense. [130]

Politicians and the media sow the seeds of hatred with slanderous stereotypes of corrupt and lazy "welfare queens." When California cut its monthly AFDC payment for a mother and two children in 1991—which was already

$2,645 below the official annual poverty line—Governor Pete Wilson said it meant "one less six-pack per week." [131]

Contrary to "welfare mother" stereotype, the typical recipient has one or two children and "is a short-term user" of AFDC. Most families receiving AFDC are enrolled for less than two years, if single spells are considered, and less than four years in total, if multiple spells over time are considered. [132] A minority of families become long-term recipients. Long-term recipients have greater obstacles to getting off welfare, such as lacking prior work experience, a high school degree or child care, or having disabilities or poor health. Contrary to stereotype, less than 4 percent of mothers receiving AFDC are 18 or younger. [133]

Also contrary to stereotype, most daughters in families who received welfare do not become welfare recipients as adults. [134] The myth of an intergenerational Black matriarchy of "welfare queens" is particularly reprehensible since Black women were enslaved workers for over two centuries and have always had a high labor force participation rate and, because of racism and sexism, a disproportionate share of low wages and poverty. [135]

Being married is neither necessary nor sufficient to avoid poverty. The official 1993 poverty rates for married-couple families with children under 18 were 8 percent for Whites, 14 percent for Blacks, and 24 percent for Latinos. [136] As seen earlier, poverty is much greater and rising in families with married couples under 30. Still, a wave of policies under names like "wedfare" and "bridefare" is being enacted—and worse policies are being proposed—which reward women who marry and punish unmarried women and their children. A popular policy now is to deny women any increased benefits for additional children, with the long-disproven rationale that more benefits beget more children. Remember that existing benefits are already way below what the government considers necessary for subsistence, and the proportion of female-headed households was rising while AFDC benefits were plunging. We are returning to the day when states denied welfare to "illegitimate" children. Republican leaders promise to take us back to a future of orphanages and poor houses.

The welfare system of recent decades didn't create poverty, but it does minimize help and maximize humiliation. When Barbara Sobel, then head of the New York City Human Resources Administration, posed as a welfare applicant to experience the system firsthand, she was misdirected, mistreated, and so "depersonalized," she says, "I ceased to be." She remained on welfare, with a mandatory part-time job as a clerk in a city office, despite repeated pleas for full-time work, and learned that most recipients desperately want jobs.[137]

State and federal policies have imposed mandatory work and training programs for welfare recipients. A 1988 federal study estimated that there were only enough "low-skill" job openings nationwide to employ one out of six AFDC recipients who might be expected to work under the Family Support Act of 1988. Nearly 40 percent of AFDC families have at least one child two years old or younger. In a discriminatory, dangerous move to expand day care for AFDC recipients on the cheap, many states are exempting child care providers from health and safety regulations or loosening them for child care under the Family Support Act.[138]

The widespread pretense that leaving welfare through "workfare," by whatever name, means leaving poverty and necessarily benefits children, undermines efforts to make work fair and supportive of all families by providing adequate jobs, wages, paid family leave, child care, health care, training, unemployment compensation, and so on. As the American Friends Service Committee stated in an earlier report, "Workfare. . . creates second class workers, whose situation is close to slavery. It uses these workers as an instrument for driving down wages and weakening organized labor." Schwarz and Volgy calculated that "the total number of adults who remain poor despite normally working full-time is nearly 10 million—more than double the number of adults on welfare."[139]

Unreversed Discrimination

Education is often portrayed as the great ladder out of poverty, and some-times it is. But educational opportunity is skewed by race and class, and racism and sexism undercut earnings at different levels of educational attainment. The so-called public school system is heavily weighted against low-income students because of reliance on property taxes for funding. Four decades after the Supreme Court outlawed school segregation, children of color are often severely deprived of school resources and positive reinforcement in an "educational" system characterized by "savage inequalities." [140]

In a school system rigged in favor of the already-privileged, some kids are tracked for success, others for failure. They are tracked by school, within school, and within the classroom. "American children in general—and Black children in particular—are rated, sorted, and boxed like so many potatoes moving down a conveyer belt," observes social psychologist Jeff Howard. "There is the 'gifted and talented' or advanced placement track for those few (exceedingly few when it comes to Black children) considered highly intelligent. There are the regular programs for those of more modest endowment, and the vocational or special education classes for those considered 'slow.' Only children in the gifted programs can expect the kind of education that will give them access to the challenges and rewards of the 21st century. Placement in vocational or special education programs is tantamount to a sentence of economic marginality at best." Howard points out, "Black students make up 16 percent of public school students, yet make up almost 40 percent of those placed in special education or classified as mentally retarded or disabled. They are even more severely under-represented in the upper end of the placement hierarchy." [141]

Jeannie Oakes, author of *Keeping Track: How Schools Structure Inequality*, found that youngsters of color "were consistently assigned to lower tracks even when they had higher test scores than White youngsters who were placed in the highest tracks." [142] Deborah Prothrow-Stith, assistant dean of the Harvard School of Public Health, observes, "Social scientists and educators have proven time and again that children tend to perform academically as they are expected to perform. By and large, children who are expected by their parents and their teachers to work hard and achieve, do just that... Children who are labelled as 'C' students, tend to do 'C' work." The negative reinforcement given many children of color in school is part of a process that Jeff Howard calls "spirit murder." [143]

Despite continued discrimination in school resources and expectations, Blacks ages 25 to 29 (a useful measure of recent educational attainment trends) have almost closed the once-wide gap with Whites on high school graduation rates—83 percent for Blacks, 87 percent for Whites—and narrowed it for those with at least a college bachelor's degree, though there the artificial gap remains wide—13 percent for Blacks, 25 percent for Whites. The respective rates for Latinos are much lower—61 percent and 8 percent—reflecting such factors as discrimination and immigration. [144]

Skyrocketing tuition and educational cutbacks are undermining progress for people of color and all those with lower incomes at a time when a college degree is increasingly essential for decent earnings. "Even as a good education has become the litmus test in the job market," says *Business Week*, "the widening wage chasm has made it harder for lower-income people to get to college. Kids from the top income quarter have had no problem: 76 percent earn bachelor's degrees today, versus 31 percent in 1980. But less than 4 percent of those in bottom-quarter families now finish college, versus 6 percent then." According to a congressionally-mandated commission, "in the 1980s, the cost of attending a private college or university soared 146 percent—a higher rate than medical, home, food, and car costs." But between 1980 and 1990, federal financial aid rose only 47 percent, says the independent college association. As reported by *Business Week*, "Tuition at public colleges, where 80 percent of students go, jumped an inflation-adjusted 49 percent in the 1980s, to $1,900 a year, according to a study by Harvard University economist Thomas J. Kane. With room and board, the tab will run to $5,400—an amount families should be expected to pay only if they earn $52,000 a year, according to federal guidelines. Meanwhile, Pell grants—the federal program that gives an average of $1,500 a year to more than a quarter of the country's 14 million college students—trailed inflation by 13 percent in the 1980s." [145]

Today's college students are working longer hours at jobs while in school and have more debt when they graduate. They are typically older and take five or six years to graduate because of such factors as work demands and not enough space in courses needed for graduation because of cutbacks. According to Northeastern University's Center for Labor Market Studies, "less than one-third of all college undergraduates complete their education in the four years after high school—compared to 45.4 percent in 1977." [146]

For people of color, discrimination is compounded by insult. It's common for people of color to get none of the credit when they succeed—portrayed as undeserving beneficiaries of affirmative action and "reverse discrimination"—and all of the blame when they fail. For centuries, there were virtual quotas of zero for people of color in top universities, higher paid industries, and government. As discrimination persists, many Whites are saying that "reverse discrimination" is a larger problem than racism. A study of the views of 15- to 24-year-olds found that 49 percent of Whites believe that it is more likely that "qualified Whites lose out on scholarships, jobs, and promotions because minorities get special preferences" than that "qualified minorities are denied scholarships, jobs, and promotions because of racial prejudice." Only 34 percent believed that minorities are more likely to lose out. Many Whites voiced racist stereotypes. [147]

In 1992, the Massachusetts Commission Against Discrimination became the nation's first state-sponsored program to use testers to assess employment discrimination. As reported in the *Boston Globe*, "Although they were strangers, Quinn O'Brien and Darryl Vance had much in common. Both were handsome, articulate undergraduates with ambition. Vance had his eye on medical school; O'Brien was prelaw." They were among six students trained as employment testers. The Canadian O'Brien, who is White, was a junior at Boston College. Vance, who is Black, was a junior at Northeastern University. Vance was given better educational and employment credentials for the testing. O'Brien received many job offers while Vance's offers were scarcer and for less money and fewer benefits. [148]

The State of Working America reports that a Black worker with less than nine years' experience earned 16.4 percent less in 1989 than an equivalent White worker (in terms of experience, education, region, and so on). The gap has widened greatly since 1973, when Blacks earned 10.3 percent less, and 1979, when Blacks earned 10.9 percent less. "In terms of education, the greatest increase in the Black-White earnings gap was among college gradu-

Table 14
Official Youth Unemployment Rates, Third Quarter 1994
not seasonally adjusted

	All Races	White	Black	Latino
Ages 16–19	16.3	13.5	32.7	23.8
Male	17.2	14.2	34.6	25.9
Female	15.3	12.7	30.6	21.1
Ages 20-24	9.5	7.9	18.9	12.7
Male	9.3	7.9	18.5	11.4
Female	9.8	7.9	19.4	15.2

Note: Remember these rates only count people who have searched for work within the last four weeks.
Source: Bureau of Labor Statistics, *Employment and Earnings*, Third Quarter 1994, Table D-16.

ates, with a small 2.5 percent differential in 1979 exploding to 15.5 percent in 1989." [149]

While official unemployment rates are high for White young people, they are much higher for Blacks and Latinos (see table 14). Using carefully matched and trained pairs of White and Black young men applying for entry-level jobs, the Urban Institute documented in 1991 that discrimination against Black job seekers is "entrenched and widespread." An earlier study documented discrimination against Latinos. [150]

During the official recession of July 1990 to March 1991, Blacks were hit hardest. According to the *Wall Street Journal*, Black workers "lost a disproportionately high share of jobs in companies that cut staff, but also gained a disproportionately low share of positions added during the recession." Many lost their jobs despite having seniority. At Digital Equipment Corporation, for example, Blacks made up under 7 percent of the work force in 1990 and bore 11 percent of the layoffs by 1991. At BankAmerica, Blacks were under 8 percent of the work force and bore 28 percent of the job losses. [151]

The federal government has also been "downsizing" with discriminatory impact on Blacks. During 1992 the federal government fired Black workers at more than twice the rate of Whites. The *San Jose Mercury News* editorialized, "It's not that they have less education, experience, or seniority. The difference has nothing to do with job performance. A new federally sponsored study shows that Blacks are fired more often because of their skin color." Blacks, who were 17 percent of the executive branch workforce in

Table 15
Estimated Effects of Unemployment and Poverty
on Social Stressors, 1975–90

Percent Rise in	Effect of a 1% Rise in Unemployment	Effect of a 0.5% Rise in Poverty
Mortality		
Heart attack	2.2	ns
Stroke	1.9	ns
Crime		
Homicide	5.6	2.8
Aggravated Assault	1.8	2.9
Forcible Rape	1.9	1.5
Larceny/Theft	2.7	1.3
Robbery	1.7	2.8
Burglary	3.7	2.0

Note: ns means not significant.
Source: Mishel and Bernstein, *The State of Working America 1994–95*, Table 1.37, citing Merva and Fowles (1994)

1992, were 39 percent of those dismissed. Whites were 72 percent of the workforce and only 48 percent of those fired. (Latinos and Asians were fired at roughly the same rates as Whites.) "Rank didn't help. Black senior managers went out the door as often as Black clerks. . . It gets worse. The deck is stacked against fired minority workers with legitimate grounds for reinstatement, the study shows. They win only one in every 100 appeals."

The *Mercury News* observed, "That racial discrimination against Blacks persists is not surprising. But it is when it happens at such an obscene level in federal employment. The feds wrote the book on equal opportunity and employment. If they can't apply the rules at home, how can they enforce them elsewhere?" [152]

The top rungs of U.S. corporations are almost exclusively White and male—fictional advertisement and TV diversity notwithstanding. Discrimination against women is pervasive from the bottom to the top of the pay scale, and not because women are on the "mommy track." *Fortune* reports "that at the same level of management, the typical woman's pay is lower than her male colleague's—even when she has the exact same qualifications, works just as many years, relocates just as often, provides the main financial support for her family, takes no time off for personal reasons, and wins the same number of promotions to comparable jobs." A national survey of senior executives found that in the 1980s, women increased their minuscule share of top corporate positions from .5 to 3 percent, while Blacks (men and women) inched from .2 to .6 percent, and Latino/as from .1 to .4 percent.[153]

The false charge of "reverse discrimination" provides scapegoats, rather than solutions, for the economic distress being felt by more men and women of all races. A recent Times-Mirror poll underscores the polarizing impact of years of top-down scapegoating during hard economic times. For the first time in seven years of Times-Mirror polling, a majority of Whites—51 percent—say they agree that equal rights have been pushed too far—up from 42 percent in 1992.[154]

Locking Up "Surplus" Labor

The fact that the legal order not only countenanced but sustained slavery, segregation, and discrimination for most of our Nation's history—and the fact that the police were bound to uphold that order—set a pattern for police behavior and attitudes toward minority communities that has persisted until the present day. That pattern includes the idea that minorities have fewer civil rights, that the task of the police is to keep them under control, and that the police have little responsibility for protecting them from crime within their communities.

—"The Evolving Strategy of Police: A Minority View,"
U.S. Department of Justice, 1990. [155]

In an unusual editorial shortly after the Los Angeles riots, the *New York Times* quoted a 1990 report by the Correctional Association of New York and the New York State Coalition for Criminal Justice: "It is no accident that our correctional facilities are filled with African-American and Latino youths out of all proportion. . . Prisons are now the last stop along a continuum of injustice for these youths that literally starts before birth." The *Times* observes, "It costs about $25,000 a year to keep a kid in prison [not counting the high cost of prison construction]. That's more than the Job Corps, or college." The *Times* concludes, "There's nothing inherently criminal in young Black men of the 1990s any more than there was in young immigrant men of the 1890s. What is criminal is to write them off, fearfully, blind to the knowledge that thousands can be saved, from lives of crime and for lives of dignity." [156]

Even before the prison expansion and harsher sentences endorsed in the 1994 Crime Bill, the United States had the world's second highest imprisonment rate (following Russia). Some 1.3 million people are incarcerated in the United States at a yearly cost of nearly $27 billion.[157] The federal and state prison populations swelled 188 percent between 1980 and 1993—though, contrary to common belief, the crime rate generally went down in that period.[158] The federal prison population is more than half Black and

Latino. The state prison population was 35 percent White, 46 percent Black, and 17 percent Latino as of 1991. Between 1988 and 1992, the number of Blacks entering state prison increased 42 percent, twice the rate of Whites.[159] The racially-biased "War on Drugs," discussed below, is increasingly responsible.

The United States imprisons Black males at a rate more than four times higher than that of South Africa under apartheid. The number of Black males in prisons and jails in the United States (583,000) is greater than the number of Black males enrolled in higher education (537,000). The annual incarceration cost, an estimated $11.6 billion, is about the same as the combined federal 1994 budget for all low-income employment programs, community development grants, and Head Start.

The Washington-based Sentencing Project found that on an average day in 1989, one out of four Black men in their twenties was in prison or jail, on probation, or on parole. The comparable figure for Latino males was one in ten, and for White males, one in sixteen. Women's rates were much lower, but the racial disproportions were parallel.[160] Other studies found that on an average day in 1991, 42 percent of Black males ages 18 to 35 living in Washington, and 56 percent of those living in Baltimore, were either in jail or prison, on probation or parole, out on bond awaiting disposition of criminal charges, or being sought on an arrest warrant. The great majority of arrests were not for violent crimes. If present policies continue, some three out of four Black males in the nation's capital will be arrested and imprisoned at least once between the ages of 18 and 35.[161] A hard search for a job becomes even harder after you have a criminal record on your résumé.

There is a national pattern of racial persecution under the guise of policing and prosecution. Former Los Angeles Police Department Chief Daryl Gates acknowledged, "I think people believe that the only strategy we have is to put a lot of police officers on the street and harass people and make arrests for inconsequential things. Well, that's part of the strategy, no question about it."[162] The *Boston Globe* ran an article titled, "GUILTY. . . of being Black: Black men say success doesn't save them from being suspected, harassed, and detained." The article, which came on the heels of the Los Angeles Rodney King case, began, "They are among Boston's most accomplished citizens. They each have a story to tell about being viewed suspiciously by salespeople, bank clerks, or police. . . The incidents are frighteningly common." Harvard Law School Professor Charles Ogletree says he has "encounters with police almost annually." He worries about his son. "It scares the hell out of me when I think that there is little I can do to ensure his safety, because the police don't see him as a person. They see him as a statistic, one they equate with crime." [163]

Studies have found that people of color experience overcharges at arrest and disproportionately high bail even for minor offenses, and "detainees are more likely to be indicted, convicted, and sentenced more harshly than released defendants." [164] A study of California, Michigan, and Texas found that controlling "for relevant variables influential in sentencing. . . Blacks and Hispanics were more likely to be sentenced to prison, with longer sentences, and less likely to be accorded probation than White felony offenders." [165]

It is impossible to understand why so many people of color, particularly Blacks, have a record—and why so many more will get a record—without understanding the racially-based "War on Drugs." Three out of four drug users are White (non-Latino), but Blacks are much more likely to be arrested and convicted for drug offenses and receive harsher sentences. [166] The share of those convicted of a drug offense in the federal prison system skyrocketed from 16 percent of inmates in 1970, to 38 percent in 1986, and 61 percent in 1993—and is expected to grow to 72 percent by 1997. The percentage of drug offenders in state prisons grew from 6 percent in 1979, to 9 percent in 1986, to 21 percent in 1991; among women state prisoners, a third are serving time for drug offenses. Many of those serving time for drug charges are nonviolent, low-level offenders with no prior criminal records. The overall arrest rate for drug possession is twice as high as for sale and/or manufacturing. In 1992, 40 percent of those arrested on illicit drug charges were Black—up from 30 percent in 1984. [167] In New York City in 1989, an astounding 92 percent of people arrested for drug offenses were Black or Latino. [168] Nationally, drug arrests skyrocketed by 78 percent for juveniles of color from 1986 to 1991, while *decreasing* by a third for other juveniles. [169]

A *USA Today* special report found that Blacks were four times more likely than Whites to be arrested on drug charges in 1991.

> The war on drugs has, in many places, been fought mainly against Blacks. In every part of the country—from densely packed urban neighbor-

hoods to sprawling new suburbs, amid racial turmoil and racial calm—
Blacks are arrested at rates sometimes wildly disproportionate to those of
Whites. . .

Tens of thousands of arrests—mostly in the inner-city—resulted from
dragnets with paramilitary names. Operation Pressure Point in New York
City. Operation Thunderbolt in Memphis. Operation Hammer in Los Angeles.

But largely lost in law enforcement's antidrug fervor, critics say, is the
fact that most drug users are White. . .

[Police officials] say Blacks are arrested more frequently because drug
use often is easier to spot in the Black community, with dealing on urban
street corners. . . rather than behind closed doors.

And, the police officials say, it's cheaper to target in the Black community.

"We don't have Whites on corners selling drugs. . . They're in houses
and offices," says police chief John Dale of Albany, N.Y., where Blacks are
eight times as likely as Whites to be arrested for drugs. . . "We're locking
up kids who are scrambling for crumbs, not the people who make big
money." [170]

While the deepening economic depression for youth of color has intensified the pull of the underground drug economy, many of the easily spotted
street corner buyers are White, as are many of the "big money" traffickers
and money launderers. You don't have to be dealing or buying on street
corners to feel the racial bias of the "drug war." A study in the *New England*
Journal of Medicine found both racial and economic bias in the reporting of
pregnant women to authorities for drug or alcohol abuse, under a mandatory reporting law. The study found that substance abuse rates were slightly
higher for pregnant White women than for pregnant Black women, but
Black women were about ten times more likely to be reported to authorities; the bias was evident whether they received their prenatal care from
private doctors or public health clinics. Poor women were also more likely
to be reported. [171]

A report to Congress by the U.S. Sentencing Commission found that
most federal mandatory minimum penalties were never or rarely used, with
the most glaring exception of drug violations, and one-third of mandatory
minimum defendants had no prior criminal record. Of those convicted with
mandatory sentences, 64 percent were Black or Latino. The Commission
concluded, "The disparate application of mandatory minimum sentences,
in cases in which available data strongly suggest that a mandatory mini-

mum is applicable, appears to be related to the race of the defendant, where Whites are more likely than non-Whites to be sentenced below the applicable mandatory minimum."[172] The racial bias of the "drug war" is symbolized by the much harsher mandatory minimums for crack cocaine (mostly Blacks arrested) than powder cocaine (mostly Whites arrested).[173] And by the much more lenient and, often, treatment-oriented approach to drunk drivers, most of whom are White males. You would never know that almost the same number of people are killed annually by drunk drivers as are murdered, and alcohol is associated with more violence and homicides nationally than illicit drugs.[174]

The courts, juvenile facilities, jails, and prisons are jammed. Violent offenders are being released early to make way for nonviolent ones.[175] "Corrections" spending is consuming tax dollars that once went to social services. California, for example, spent 10 percent of its state budget on higher education in fiscal year 1983–84 and 4 percent on corrections. In fiscal year 1994–95, higher education and corrections were each allocated 10 percent.[176] The 1994 Crime Bill, capitalizing on the misconception that crime rates are soaring, will only make the situation worse, with its intensification of punishment at the expense of rehabilitation and prevention.

Cycle of Unequal Opportunity

We hear a lot about the supposed underclass "cycle of dependency." Not about the upper-class cycle of dependency on unequal opportunity. When it comes to who gets what from government, language helps discriminate. Labor, women, and people of color are called "special interests" though together they are the great majority of the population. The private, profit-making interest of corporations substitutes for the "national interest."

"Welfare" has become synonymous with AFDC—Aid to Families with Dependent Children—and transformed from a positive into a negative term. The much greater public subsidies, lucrative government contracts, and tax "incentives" for private corporations are not called "Aid For Dependent Corporations." [177] The plentiful forms of "welfare for the well-off," such as much-abused subsidies for "business" meals, travel, and mortgage interest deductions on luxury homes, are not called food and housing handouts. [178] Land plundered from Mexico is called Texas and California—while undocumented Mexican immigrants are called illegal aliens. When Native Americans were dispossessed of land and life, *they* were called savages. The long trail of broken treaties is camouflaged with terms like "Indian giver." Redlining, which siphons the savings and pensions of people of color into investment in whiter, higher-income areas, is not called looting. Discriminatory pay for women and people of color is not called robbery.

Instead of equal rights, much less reparations, former slaves and their descendants got apartheid and continued discrimination. Affirmative action has been twisted to slander people of color as subpar beneficiaries of "reverse discrimination." Meanwhile, without stigma, there is de facto affirmative action for White and wealthier alumni offspring who don't otherwise meet college "standards" despite their more privileged backgrounds. A *Boston Globe* article on so-called "legacy admissions" noted that the acceptance rate for children of Harvard alumni was more than double the rate for all applicants, class of 1992. "Far from being more qualified, or even equally qualified, the average admitted legacy at Harvard between 1981 and 1988 was significantly *less* qualified than the average nonlegacy." [179]

A long history of government welfare, such as the Homestead Act, seg-regated housing subsidies, and ongoing federal land, mineral, and timber giveaways, is rewritten as "pulling yourself up by your own bootstraps." As the story of right-wing Texas Senator Phil Gramm illustrates, welfare takes many forms: "Born in Georgia in 1942, to a father who was living on a veterans disability pension, Gramm attended a publicly funded university on a grant paid for by the federal War Orphans Act. His graduate work was financed by a National Defense Education Act fellowship, and his first job was at Texas A&M University, a federal land-grant institution." [180]

It is estimated that "since 1960, around 80 percent of social-welfare ex-penditures have been in programs not focused exclusively on the poor. . . A continuing measure of the two-tier nature of the income support system lies in the fact that Social Security was indexed for inflation in 1972, while Aid to Families with Dependent Children was not." [181] Social Security payments are based on a worker's wage record in covered employment, which reflects sex and race discrimination. Moreover, because of shorter life expectancies than their White counterparts, Black men and women benefit less from Social Security. As of 1990, "one of every three 45-year-old African Ameri-can men will die without seeing a single Social Security check; the compa-rable figure for White men is one in six." [182] The challenge for society is to assure Social Security for everyone—from children to the elderly.

The cycle of unequal opportunity has been reinforced by tax cuts re-warding the wealthy and ballooning the national debt. According to Robert Reich, now U.S. secretary of labor, "Were the tax code as progressive as it was even as late as 1977," the top 10 percent of income earners "would have paid approximately $93 billion more in taxes" than they paid in 1989.[183] How much is $93 billion? About the same amount as the combined 1989 budget for all these programs for low-income persons: AFDC ($19.7 bil-lion); Supplemental Security Income, SSI ($15.8 billion); food benefits ($22 billion), including food stamps, school lunch program, WIC (supple-mental nutrition program for pregnant and nursing Women, Infants, and Children); housing benefits, including low-rent public housing, lower-in-come housing assistance, etc. ($15.9 billion); jobs and employment train-ing ($3.9 billion); education aid, including Head Start, college loans, etc. ($13 billion); and General Assistance ($2.8 billion).[184]

Corporate taxes are way down. The share that corporate income taxes contribute to federal spending dropped from an average of 23 percent during the 1960s, to about 8 percent during much of the 1980s. "How much more would corporations have contributed each year during the 1980s had their 1970s average tax rate not been cut but merely stayed constant? $130 billion!" [185]

Lower-income taxpayers pay for the debt they didn't create with cutbacks and less-talked-about tax hikes. Payroll taxes, which are regressive because they tax the poor proportionately more than the rich, are up. The Social Security tax, collected on salaries up to a cap ($60,600 in 1994), increased 31 percent from 1977 to 1990, when the rate reached 7.65 percent.[186] Up also are regressive state and local sales and property taxes, in part because the federal government has shifted billions of dollars in costs to state and local governments. Making things still worse, state and local governments are rushing to expand lotteries, casinos, and other government-promoted gambling to raise revenues, again disproportionately from those with lower incomes, which they should be raising from fair taxes.[187]

Clinton's tax reforms went a step in the right direction by cutting income taxes on average for low-income people by expanding the Earned Income Tax Credit and raising income taxes for higher income people. But the wealthiest 1 percent of families can still expect to pay about 8 percent less in 1995 federal taxes than would have been the case under 1977 rules. The top personal income tax bracket of 39.6 percent still "remains well below the average top rate, 47 percent, charged by the 86 countries with an income tax." Moreover, capital gains are taxed at only 28 percent, substantial investment interest is tax-exempt, and the wealthy benefit disproportionately from mortgage interest and other deductions.[188] Republicans want to cut the capital gains tax in half.

And what about charitable giving? While the rich were getting richer, they were also getting stingier. In the 1980s, for all wage groups who itemized deductions on their tax returns, the average charitable contributions increased by over 9 percent; average contributions by those with pretax incomes above $1 million *decreased* by nearly 39 percent, adjusting for inflation. Charitable contributions by millionaires declined from about 7 percent of income in 1979 to below 4 percent of income in 1991. Indeed, as a percent of income, those with the least give the most.[189]

Robert Reich has warned of the "secession of the successful." He wrote that the wealthy top fifth "is quietly seceding from the rest of the nation." They have withdrawn "their dollars from the support of public spaces and institutions shared by all and dedicated the savings to their own private services"—from schools to security guards to walled-off residential communities.[190]

Disinvestment and Misinvestment

Reflecting on the 1992 Los Angeles riots, Congresswoman Maxine Waters (D-CA) quoted Robert Kennedy's words from 1968: "There is another kind of violence in America, slower but just as deadly, destructive as the shot or bomb in the night. . . This is the violence of institutions; indifference and inaction and slow decay. This is the violence that afflicts the poor, that poisons relations between men and women because their skin is different colors. This is the slow destruction of a child by hunger, and schools without books, and homes without heat in the winter." Waters added, "What a tragedy it is that America has still. . . not learned such an important lesson." [191]

In the words of the Children's Defense Fund, every day in the United States, "9 children are murdered, 13 children die from guns, 27 children— a classroom—die from poverty. . . 101 babies die before their first birthday." [192]

The Washington-based Milton S. Eisenhower Foundation was created, in part, by members and staff of President Johnson's National Advisory Commission on Civil Disorders, known as the Kerner Commission. It was following the 1968 riots that the Kerner Commission issued its famous warning that the United States was becoming "two societies, one Black, one White—separate and unequal." Twenty-five years later, the Eisenhower Foundation issued a report concluding: "Overall, in spite of some gains since the 1960s, but especially because of the federal disinvestments of the 1980s, the famous prophesy of the Kerner Commission. . . is more relevant today than in 1968, and more complex, with the emergence of multiracial disparities and growing income segregation."

In the words of the Eisenhower Foundation report, "Federal tax and income policy that helped the rich was accompanied by federal disinvestment policy that hurt the poor. . . From 1980 to 1990, federal community development block grants to the cities were cut from over $6B [billion] to under $3B." Moreover, "from 1979 to 1990, overall federal outlays on defense skyrocketed, from close to $200B per year to nearly $300B per year, while overall federal outlays for education, job training, employment, and social services declined from over $50B per year to under $40B per year—an astounding drop of over twenty percent. . . The huge military increases were financed only in a small way by the domestic cuts. Most was paid for by running up the national debt." The Eisenhower Foundation adds:

> One exception to the federal government's domestic disinvestment was prison building. . . costing $37B at the federal and state levels over the decade. . . Because the inmates were disproportionately young, in many ways prison building became the American youth policy of choice over the mid 1980s and early 1990s. . . [Because they were disproportionately youth of color], in some ways prison building became part of the nation's civil rights policy. Given that the population in American prisons more than doubled over the decade, while funding for housing for the poor was cut, incredibly, by more than eighty percent from 1978 to 1991 [after accounting for inflation], and given that the cost of a new prison cell in New York State was about the average cost of a new home purchased in the United States nationally, in some ways prison building became the American low-income housing policy of the 1980s.[193]

Just as conservatives intended, the federal budget deficit—produced by skyrocketing military spending and tax cuts favoring the wealthy (who profit from the interest paid on debt financing)—has been used as a permanent enforcer of cutbacks in social spending. Clinton's campaign program to "Rebuild America" and "put people first" was quickly sacrificed on the altar of deficit reduction. Behind the headlines about new commitments to Head Start, for example, overall education and training spending declined.[194]

We have a greed surplus and a justice deficit. New federal priorities are not a matter of wallet, but will. For example, as *The State of Working America* reports, the United States spends proportionately much less than European countries in "the provision of publicly provided job training, job creation, and subsidies. Such programs are vital in an economy experiencing a shift from manufacturing to services and a reduction in the size of the armed forces." In 1991-92, the U.S. government spent only 0.09 percent of Gross Domestic Product (GDP) on job training and placement, and direct job creation and subsidies. The percentage in other OECD countries ranged from 0.17 to 1.45 percent.[195]

In 1992 the United States spent four times more on the military than the federal government invested in education, job training, housing, economic development, and environmental protection combined. The U.S. share of world military spending was an incredible 42.5 percent[196] (see table 16). The 1993 military budget of $291 billion was 20 percent higher, adjusting for inflation, than the Cold War budget of 1980. In the words of the Washington-based Center for Defense Information (CDI), led by retired military officers, the Clinton "Administration wants to spend an astounding $1.3 Trillion on the military over a period of just five years. In the final year of the plan, the downward trend will be reversed as military spending rises again." CDI warns that "Pentagon five-year plans have long been grounded in overstated threats and understated costs." It urges politicians not to rationalize military spending as "a welfare program," noting, "money spent on real needs will generate more jobs than are currently wasted on unneeded military programs." [197] Republicans promise to spend even more on the military.

Instead of stopping production of unnecessary new weapons systems and supporting serious military-civilian conversion at home and abroad, the U.S. government is reinforcing militarism by avidly expanding weapons exports. The United States is the world's leading arms dealer and, in 1993, "about three-quarters of these sales went to governments deemed repressive or undemocratic in the State Department's own human rights reports." Behind the rhetoric about economic benefits, "William Hartung of the World Policy Institute found that when subsidies and indirect costs are factored in, 'the net value of arms exports to the U.S. economy in a given year will range somewhere between a small net gain and a small net loss.' " [198] The real costs are even greater in terms of polluted and wasted resources, weapons proliferation, and violated human rights.

Numerous military and foreign policy specialists have called for bringing the military budget down to $175 billion or less by the end of the decade, including the Center for Defense Information (CDI), former Secretary of Defense Robert McNamara, and defense analyst William Kaufman. Arms control expert Randall Forsberg, director of the Institute for Defense and Disarmament Studies, goes much further. She proposes a phased ten-year program to build a cooperative international security system with strong mechanisms for peaceful conflict resolution and a commitment to "non-offensive defense," bringing the U.S. military budget to $87 billion, for savings of $989 billion.[199] To reduce the military budget to that level and lower, the United States has to willfully commit itself to fostering international demilitarization and nonviolent conflict resolution. We must make that commitment now. As Martin Luther King warned in *Where Do We Go From Here,* "A nation that continues year after year to spend more money on military defense than on programs of social uplift is approaching spiritual death."

Figure 6
Comparative Military Spending, 1993
in $billions

United States	291	
Japan	40	
France	36	
United Kingdom	35	
Germany	31	
Russia	29	
China*	22	
Italy	17	
Saudi Arabia	16	
South Korea	12	
Combined Iraq, Iran, Libya, Syria and North Korea†	22	

*1992 figure. Source: Center for Defense Information, "1995 Military Spending: The Real Story," *The Defense Monitor* XXIII:5 (1994).
† 1992 figures. Source: National Priorities Project, *In Search of Security*, 1994.

Unfair and Unsustainable Development

As others have noted, unrestrained growth is the ideology of the cancer cell.

—Muhammad Yunus, "Redefining Development" [200]

The rapacious global corporate model of development exploits and endangers both people and environment. "The North, with 20 percent of world population, uses up 80 percent of world resources and has a per capita income on average 15 times higher than that of the South," writes economist Martin Khor Kok Peng, editor of *Third World Resurgence* and director of the Malaysia-based Third World Network. There is a "socio-ecological crisis." As the earth's resources are exhausted and contaminated, "much of the world's output and income are channeled to a small elite (mostly in the North but also in the South), while a large part of humanity (mostly in the South, but also a growing minority in the North) has insufficient means to satisfy its needs." [201]

According to the UN Development Program, "During the past five decades, world income increased sevenfold (in real GDP) and income per person more than tripled (in per capita GDP). But this gain has been spread very unequally—nationally and internationally—and the inequality is increasing. Between 1960 and 1991, the share of world income for the richest 20 percent of the global population rose from 70 percent to 85 percent. Over the same period, all but the richest quintile saw their share of world income fall—and the meager share for the poorest 20 percent declined from 2.3 percent to 1.4 percent." In 1960, the richest 20 percent of the world's population had 30 times as much income as the poorest 20 percent. By 1991, the richest 20 percent had 61 times as much income as the poorest 20 percent. [202]

To "develop" their countries as cash-crop plantations and export-platforms for global corporations, Western-backed Third World regimes—many of them autocratic—went into heavy debt with multinational banks and agencies such as the International Monetary Fund (IMF) and the World Bank. Like international loan sharks, the bankers encourage them to rob their people to service the debt—a debt used to enrich local and foreign elites.

This so-called development financing has been politically, economically, socially, and ecologically disastrous. Governments attempting to better serve their poor majorities were punished with lending blockades or forced to accept IMF and World Bank "adjustment" programs, which demand local currency devaluations, encouragement of foreign investment, reduced government spending on social services, curtailment of food and other basic necessity subsidies, higher interest rates and taxes, lower wages, deregulation, and privatization.

Women are disproportionately hurt by structural adjustment programs. Even AID acknowledges this: "Women have been forced to act as 'shock absorbers' for structural adjustment." They have disproportionately experienced public sector layoffs and cutbacks in health care, education, and so on. "Many women now work 60 to 90 hours per week just to maintain the marginal standard of living they possessed a decade ago." [203]

In *The State of the World's Children 1989*, UNICEF observed: "Throughout most of Africa and much of Latin America, average incomes have fallen by 10 percent to 25 percent in the 1980s. In the 37 poorest nations, spending per head on health has been reduced by 50 percent, and on education by 25 percent." Taking into account aid, repayments of interest and capital, and the unequal terms of trade between the North's manufactured goods and the South's raw materials, "then the annual flow from the poor to the rich might be as much as $60 billion each year." [204]

In UNICEF's words, "Hundreds of thousands of the developing world's children have given their lives to pay their countries' debts, and many millions more are still paying the interest with their malnourished minds and bodies." UNICEF estimates that about 500,000 children die yearly from austerity measures mandated because of the debt. [205] It is time to recognize that the Third World "debt" has been more than repaid through colonialism, neocolonialism, and usurious interest.

The General Agreement on Tariffs and Trades (GATT) is another cornerstone of global corporate domination. Even more than the North American

Free Trade Agreement (NAFTA), GATT and its successor World Trade Organization will undermine small farmers, speed up ecological crises, and threaten the health and safety of workers and consumers. It will deepen Third World dependence, reward the production of cash crops for export over food needed for local consumption, and tighten corporate control over culture, technology, and resources, including seeds and medicinal plants. With the new GATT and regional Free Trade Agreements, corporations will be freer to exploit workers, consumers, and the environment throughout the world.

Meanwhile, an international elite of financial investors and speculators is using the latest computer capabilities to electronically sweep the world for ready profit, often at the expense of long-run investment, not to mention workers' livelihoods. Former Citicorp chair Walter Wriston has boasted that "200,000 monitors in trading rooms all over the world" now conduct "a kind of global plebiscite on the monetary and fiscal policies of the governments issuing currency. . . There is no way for a nation to opt out." [206] No way, that is, under the rigged rules of corporate domination.

Working as a janitor in downtown Washington, D.C., [Maria Elena Flores, an immigrant from El Salvador] earns the D.C. minimum wage ($4.75 an hour) and has no health insurance. To make ends meet, she shares a small apartment with three other adults.

"The pay is not much," she said. . . "and if you are one minute late, they take away money."

The building Flores works to clean five nights a week is one of several housing the Washington headquarters of the International Bank for Reconstruction and Development—better known as the World Bank. . .

The people whose offices Flores cleans have good jobs. They are engineers, economists, and technical experts. . . They come from all over the world. Their pay is generous, and so are their benefits and health coverage. . .

There are about 250 janitors who clean the Bank's office buildings. They, too, come from all over the world—from Ghana, Egypt, Brazil, Jamaica, Sierra Leone, Nigeria, as well as from El Salvador and the United States. Most are women. And, like Flores, many are from countries to which the Bank has made development loans.

Employed by a private cleaning contractor, these janitors are offered only part-time work. Their pay averages about $115 a week, or less than $6,000 a year. This forces some of them to rely on public assistance. An example is Denise Speed, 24. While working as a janitor at the World Bank, Speed had to live in a homeless shelter for several months. Now she lives in an apartment subsidized by the D.C. government and qualifies for food stamps.

The World Bank janitors are overwhelmingly in favor of a campaign for union representation begun in 1988 by SEIU (Services Employees International Union) Local 525 in Washington. (The Bank used to have a unionized cleaning contractor, but changed to a nonunion contractor several years ago.). . . [World Bank officials] indicated that, should the cleaning firm sign a union contract with the janitors, the Bank might switch to another cleaning company. In addition to union recognition, the janitors have sought a pay increase to $6.50 an hour, health insurance, paid sick days, and holidays. . .

At one point, eight [prounion] protestors were arrested in a peaceful sit-in demonstration at the Bank building's main entrance. But the janitors and their union haven't given up.

—Margie Snider,
"Fighting Poverty at the World Bank," in *50 Years is Enough*

We the People: Putting Economics in Human Rights

Labor is prior to, and independent of, capital. Capital is only the fruit of labor, and could never have existed if labor had not first existed. Labor is the superior of capital, and deserves much the higher consideration.
—President Abraham Lincoln,
Message to Congress, December 3, 1861.

WE THE PEOPLE of the United States, in Order to form a more perfect Union, establish Justice, insure domestic Tranquillity, provide for the common defense, promote the general Welfare, and secure the Blessings of Liberty to ourselves and our Posterity, do ordain and establish this Constitution for the United States of America.
—*Constitution of the United States*, 1787.

Economic rights are fundamental to the establishment of Justice, Tranquillity, the promotion of the general Welfare, and securing the Blessings of Liberty for ourselves and our posterity. Economic rights are fundamental human rights. Yet a half century after President Roosevelt proposed an Economic Bill of Rights for the United States and the United Nations adopted a Declaration of Human Rights, including economic rights, the welfare and justice of people are being sacrificed to the liberty of global corporations. Two decades after the United Nations adopted a Declaration and Program of Action on the Establishment of a New International Economic Order, respecting national sovereignty and dedicated to the redress of inequalities and injustices, most of the world has come under the domain of the Global Corporate Order in which people and nations are merely means to further profit for the elite.

"Free trade" agreements such as NAFTA and GATT can be understood as economic bills of rights for corporations. We must come together nationally and internationally to promote an economic bill of rights for people. Corporations would be actors in a just economy, not its masters. Workers, women, and others must reject their dismissal by elites as "minorities" and "special interests" and claim their rightful place at the heart of the national interest. Democracy cannot survive, much less thrive, in a world where popular will is secondary to corporate power.

Speaking about his plans to end the current welfare system, President Clinton told U.S. governors in February 1993, "we will remove the incentive for staying in poverty"; people should not "draw a check for doing nothing when they can do something." We have to reject the notion of work which presumes that a mother raising a child with the help of welfare is getting something for "doing nothing," while someone managing a corporation whose toxic waste is polluting that mother's community is a productive member of society.

The Clinton administration's stated goal of insuring that no one working full-time lives below the poverty line—by raising the Earned Income Tax Credit and perhaps raising the minimum wage—is a step forward, but it does not address these realities: The poverty line is set well below actual sufficiency in basic necessities, full-time jobs are becoming scarcer, and many parents with young children cannot work full-time inside the home and full-time outside it. Like Reagan-Bushonomics, Clintonomics is generally exacerbating impoverishing trends. The Republican Contract With America is much worse.

In the United States and around the world, people are working together—acting locally, nationally, and internationally—to oppose the negative trends discussed here and promote just alternatives: from community-based organizations to cross-border coalitions and international Non-Governmental Organization (NGO) forums; from women's economic literacy and economic development projects to credit unions and environmental organizations; from urban community land trusts to agricultural cooperatives; from fair trade campaigns and consumer boycotts to alternative technology and people-to-people trading; from local campaigns to stop toxic dumping to the growing movement against environmental racism; from human rights and youth organizations to international trade unions.

In their diverse ways, these groups and movements practice solidarity. In the words of the AFSC report *From Global Pillage to Global Village*, "solidarity is the recognition that every human being has the potential to contribute to building a fairer, safer, and healthier life for all." [207] The AFSC, with its multifaceted commitment to justice and nonviolence, has long recognized the importance of understanding and challenging global corporate domination. In 1978 the AFSC Nationwide Women's Program (NWP) sponsored a groundbreaking conference on women and global corporations and, in 1990 it produced *The Global Factory: Analysis and Action for a New Economic Era* in collaboration with the Maquiladora Project of the AFSC Mexico-U.S. Border Project. The Maquiladora Project was begun in 1979, long before the debate over NAFTA drew widespread and often xenophobic attention to the operations of U.S. corporations in Mexico. The AFSC has supported numerous economic development projects in the United States and around the world—projects that demonstrate the everyday viability of alternative economic policies and practices.

Bills of economic rights have been spelled out before, as in the Roosevelt proposal, the United Nations declaration, and the International Covenant on Economic, Social, and Cultural Rights. They are being elaborated and expanded in many forums today, enriched by anti-racist, feminist, indigenous, and ecological perspectives. These initiatives take a variety of shapes, from social and environmental charters to detailed democratic and sustainable development strategies.[208] There are indeed worthy alternatives to Clinton's so-called Middle Class Bill of Rights and the Republicans' Contract With America, a contract on the American dream.

Extract from President Franklin D. Roosevelt's introduction to
an *Economic Bill of Rights*, annual message to Congress, 1944

We have come to a clear realization of the fact that true individual
freedom cannot exist without economic security and independence... We
have accepted... a second Bill of Rights under which a new basis of
security and prosperity can be established for all—regardless of station,
race, or creed.

Among these are:

The right to a useful and remunerative job...

The right to earn enough to provide adequate food and clothing and recreation...

The right of every family to a decent home;

The right to adequate medical care and the opportunity to achieve and
enjoy good health;

The right to adequate protection from the economic fears of old age, sickness, accident, and unemployment;

The right to a good education.

Universal Declaration of Human Rights,
adopted by the United Nations General Assembly, 1948

All human beings are born free and equal in dignity and rights...

Everyone has the right to work... and to protection against unemployment.

Everyone, without any discrimination, has the right to equal pay for equal
work.

Everyone who works has the right to just and favorable remuneration ensuring for himself [sic] and his family an existence worthy of human
dignity, and supplemented, if necessary, by other means of social protection.

Everyone has the right to form and to join trade unions for the protection of
his interests.

Everyone has the right to rest and leisure, including reasonable limitation
of working hours and periodic holidays with pay.

Everyone has the right to a standard of living adequate for the health and
well-being of himself and of his family, including food, clothing, housing, and medical care and necessary social services, and the right to
security in the event of unemployment, sickness, disability, widowhood,
old age, or other lack of livelihood in circumstances beyond his control...

All children, whether born in or out of wedlock, shall enjoy the same social protection...

Everyone is entitled to a social and international order in which the rights
and freedoms set forth in this Declaration can be fully realized...

Keys to the Future

To address the growing challenge of human security, a new development paradigm is needed that puts people at the center of development, regards economic growth as a means and not an end, protects the life opportunities of future generations as well as the present generations, and respects the natural systems on which all life depends.

—United Nations Development Program,
Human Development Report 1994.

We can and must invest in people, the environment, and the future. Here are key elements of national and international policies fostering fair and sustainable development.

• **All-Age Social Security.** Societies with no ceiling on the private accumulation of wealth have a special obligation to provide a solid foundation upon which all people may build. Without that foundation, there is nothing remotely approaching "equal opportunity." As Martin Luther King urged, "The time has come for us to civilize ourselves by the total, direct, and immediate abolition of poverty." We should set a realistic, basic human needs level and assure adequate income to meet it through the tax system and government programs such as universal health care. All-Age Social Security would replace piecemeal and inadequate income support programs such as AFDC.

• **Fair Taxation and Income Support.** Bring everyone's income up to the basic human needs level with a refundable tax credit (adjusted for number of dependents). Those with incomes below the basic human needs line would get a cash grant to make up the difference, payable in regular installments, whether they are in the paid workforce or not (unlike the Earned Income Tax Credit). For people with incomes above the line, the tax credit would ensure they do not fall below it after taxes; it would serve as a greatly enhanced version of the personal and dependent deductions now in existence. Restore real progressivity to the tax system by increasing the range and number of personal income tax rates, with lower bottom rates and higher top rates, indexed for inflation. The rates would reflect wide-ranging differences in income and wealth. Lower the Social Security tax rate and remove the cap on taxable income. Raise corporate taxes. It's time to stop the pretense that the rich—who hold an oligarchic share of the nation's wealth—are being drained by high taxes.

  •   **Work Fair and Full Employment.** A decent job at fair pay should be a right, not a privilege. Society can't demand that people work for a living, but deny many a living wage. Today we have the absurd situation of high unemployment at a time when millions of people need work and urgent work needs people—from repairing bridges and building mass transit, to cleaning up pollution and converting to renewable energy, to teaching and staffing after-school programs and community centers, to building and renovating affordable housing. In the words of New Initiatives for Full Employment, "a nation that intones the work ethic has the ethical obligation to provide an opportunity for gainful and productive employment to all." [209] The minimum wage must be raised and keep pace with the basic human needs level.

  •   **Shorter Hours, Share the Work.** Mandatory overtime should be prohibited and a shorter standard work week of 30 hours should be implemented. In the 1930s, U.S. labor called on the nation to "share the work." Today, Italian labor advocates *Lavorare meno, lavorare tutti*—work less and everybody works. The idea of a shorter work week is one whose time has come again. The 1993 AFL-CIO convention turned renewed attention to the issue of reduced hours. In contrast to European countries, which mandate four to five weeks of annual vacation, the United States mandates no paid vacation and averages a measly nine days. Instead of encouraging the Europeans to follow the United States and give up their social welfare advances, the United States should learn from them.

  •   **Workers' Rights.** Workers' rights include the right to a livable wage, to organize and bargain collectively, to strike without fear of permanent replacement workers, to occupational health and safety, and to participation in workplace decisions. All workers should have the same rights and benefits, be they full-time or contingent workers, domestic workers, farm workers, or others.

  •   **Environmentally Sustainable Development.** Instead of "harmonizing" standards to low common denominators in the name of "free trade," high standards would be promoted in the name of health and safety. Localities, states and nations, including indigenous nations, must have the right to establish and enforce tougher regulations on pesticides and toxic waste disposal, than those set internationally. Prohibit the export of toxic and hazardous substances that are banned in the country of origin. "The right of Nations to establish national food and agriculture policies in order to eradicate hunger and ensure food security should be explicitly recognized. There should be no patenting of life forms."[210] National and international aid and financing should encourage, rather than undermine, renewable energy, appropriate technology, and organic farming. Democratize or abolish national and international institutions, such as the anti-worker U.S. Federal Reserve Board, UN Security Council, the International Monetary Fund, World Bank, World Trade Organization. End the imposition of "structural adjustment" programs. Write off or reduce Third World debt. Respect indigenous land, water, and other resource rights.

•   **Conversion of the Military-Industrial Economy.** Give sustained support for comprehensive conversion of military and environmentally hazardous production to socially responsible uses. Sharply reduce the military budget, aiming at a true bottom-up restructuring such as the "nonoffensive defense" and cooperative security model mentioned earlier. Immediately stop the sale of military and military-related equipment to repressive regimes. Instead of maintaining interventionist militarism with the popular post-Cold War rationale of protecting jobs for defense workers, everyone should be able to count on an effective system of income support, education, and training—be they defense workers, soldiers or teachers, loggers or construction workers, computer assemblers or farm workers.

As Robert Pollin explains, "In *Making Peace With the Planet*, Barry Commoner estimated that it would cost $1 trillion—a little more than what the Pentagon spends in three years—to transform the existing production system in the United States. This would entail an epoch-defining reconstruction of our mode of production—the substitution of solar for fossil fuel energy; high performance organic farming for pesticides; and a range of alternatives for most petrochemical products... It says don't lower environmental standards to save jobs; rather, create jobs by investing in the technological transformations that will raise environmental standards."[211]

•   **Nonviolent Conflict Resolution.** Make nonviolent conflict resolution part of the core school curriculum at every grade. Support community programs dedicated to peaceful conflict resolution. Strengthen international bodies such as the International Court of Justice (World Court). End big-power domination.

- **Codes of Conduct** mandating social and ecological responsibility. To stop the "downward spiral" of city versus city, state versus state, and nation versus nation, bidding wars for business, national, and global standards should be set and enforced for minimum wages, labor practices, consumer safety, environmental regulation, and so on. No corporation should receive tax breaks or other public subsidies without adhering to standards, such as those already set by the International Labor Organization and the Generalized System of Preferences. Violations should be enforced through civil and criminal penalties. As President Roosevelt declared in a message to Congress on the 1937 Fair Labor Standards Act, the first nationally applicable law setting minimum labor standards and outlawing child labor: "Goods produced under conditions which do not meet a rudimentary standard of decency should be regarded as contraband and ought not to be able to pollute the channels of interstate commerce."[212]

- **Corporate Accountability.** As the Los Angeles-based Labor/Community Strategy Center puts it, "government funds are a public trust, and business cannot receive funds and then operate contrary to broader public interests." In exchange for public subsidies, business should accept contractual prohibitions against capital flight. If they violate these agreements, they should repay government funds.[213]

- **Community Investment and Redevelopment.** End all redlining and other discrimination by banks and insurance companies. Strengthen the Community Reinvestment Act and pass counterpart legislation for insurance companies. Secure and reinvest workers' pension funds in socially-responsible projects. Support community development banks, credit unions, and loan funds. The successful Grameen Bank of Bangladesh, for example, which lends mostly to rural women, rejected the traditional banking approach of "the more you have, the more you can borrow," and affirms instead, "the less you have, the higher your priority."[214] Provide incentives for nonprofit and democratically-controlled enterprises, such as cooperatives, employee-owned firms, community land trusts, and credit unions, including incentives for the international trade of goods and services provided by such enterprises. The focal point of the kind of financial and other assistance typically provided to corporations through "free trade zones" or domestic enterprise or "empowerment" zones—in the name of benefiting the community—should be representative community organizations, not corporations and government planners. As innovative and successful organizations like the Dudley Street Neighborhood Initiative of Boston show, there can be no community "empowerment" without organizing and community power. And without community organizing, planning and long-term control, there will be no sustainable, comprehensive community development.[215]

•   **Nondiscrimination** on the basis of race, gender, national origin, ethnicity, religion, age, disability, marital status, sexual orientation, immigration status, or political beliefs. Strong enforcement of current laws and passage of new ones.

•   **Child Caring.** Most parents work outside the home as well as inside it. Government must provide the support necessary to assure affordable, quality child care with decent wages for home and center-based providers. End the pretense that most mothers are home in the afternoon, and make after-school programs a part of every school. The United States is the only industrialized nation except Australia that doesn't provide paid and job-protected maternity leave (varying between 50 and 100 percent of salary and from 6 to 65 weeks), with most countries providing at least four months. Some countries provide paternity leave. All should.

•   **Universal Health Care.** The rationing of health care by income is unconscionable. To make matters worse, private insurance companies may deny coverage to those who most need protection because of preexisting conditions. Many nations have managed to show care for their people with a single-payer system of universal coverage. The United States should join them.

•   **Equal Educational Opportunity** from preschool to college to adult education. End the discriminatory financing of public schools through private property taxes. Schools should be better utilized as community centers for lifelong learning, culture, and recreation. Public financing should assure that no one forgoes college for economic reasons. Sabbaticals should be a right of all workers, not just those in academia.

•   **Participatory Democracy.** Make the principle of one-person, one-vote meaningful by taking the power of money out of politics. Public financing of local, state, and federal campaigns is essential. Other elements include universal voter registration and free media for in-depth debate among candidates and voters. Establish a federal Voting Day holiday to encourage maximum voting turnout and participation. Eliminate the structural biases against independents and third parties.

It is time to break the cycle of unequal opportunity. Time to stop building walls between people, and start building bridges. Time to stop scapegoating, and start solving our shared problems.

Notes

1. See Holly Sklar, *Chaos or Community? Seeking Solutions, Not Scapegoats for Bad Economics*, forthcoming South End Press, Spring 1995; "Disposable Workers," *Z Magazine*, January 1994; "The Upperclass and Mothers N the Hood," *Z Magazine*, March 1993; "Young and Guilty By Stereotype," *Z Magazine*, July/August 1993; "Brave New World Order," in Cynthia Peters, ed., *Collateral Damage: The New World Order at Home and Abroad* (Boston: South End Press, 1992).
2. Lawrence Mishel and Jared Bernstein, *The State of Working America 1994-95* (Washington, DC: Economic Policy Institute, 1994, press edition), pp. 238-40, 244, 248-49, citing reports by Edward Wolff.
3. Donald L. Barlett and James B. Steele, *America: What Went Wrong* (Kansas City: Andrews and McMeel, 1992), p. ix.
4. Editorial, "Executive Pay: It Doesn't Add Up" and "Executive Pay: The Party Ain't Over Yet," *Business Week*, April 26, 1993; "What, Me Overpaid? CEOs Fight Back," *Business Week*, May 4, 1992; Labor Research Association (New York), *American Labor Yearbook 1993*, p. 35. 1980-93 pay, price and profit comparisons from "CEO Pay Soars," *Solidarity* (UAW), September 1994.
5. "That Eye-Popping Executive Pay: Is Anybody Worth This Much?" and editorial, "CEO Pay: A Skyrocket That Could Backfire," *Business Week*, April 25, 1994.
6. Graef S. Crystal, *In Search of Excess: The Overcompensation of American Executives* (New York: W.W. Norton, 1992), pp. 23, 213.
7. Children's Defense Fund and Northeastern University's Center for Labor Market Studies, *Vanishing Dreams: The Economic Plight of America's Young Families* (Washington, DC: Children's Defense Fund, 1992), p. 22; Clifford M. Johnson et al., *Child Poverty in America* (Children's Defense Fund, 1991), pp. 13-15, 25.
8. U.S. Bureau of the Census (hereafter Census Bureau), *Studies in Household and Family Formation* (1992), pp. 29-30.
9. John E. Schwarz and Thomas J. Volgy, *The Forgotten Americans: Thirty Million Working Poor in the Land of Opportunity* (New York: W.W. Norton, 1992), pp. 38-46, 61-62 and "Above the Line—But Poor," *The Nation*, February 15, 1993. Child care figure from Children's Defense Fund, *The State of America's Children 1992*, p. 19 and other sources. Low-rent units/low-income renters figures from Center on Budget and Policy Priorities (Washington, DC), *Funding for Low-Income Programs in FY 1994*, p. 6.
10. For female-headed families with children living at 125 to 150 percent of the official poverty line, the average 1989 amount of in-kind income received in food stamps and housing assistance was $312. For male-present families with children, the average amount was $170. Schwarz and Volgy, *The Forgotten Americans*, fn. 14, pp. 178-79. Household assistance figures from Census Bureau, *Poverty in the United States: 1992 (1993)*, pp. xvii-xviii, Tables F and G, and "Health Insurance Coverage—1993," *Statistical Brief*, October 1994.
11. Isaac Shapiro and Robert Greenstein, *Selective Prosperity: Increasing Income Disparities Since 1977* (Center on Budget and Policy Priorities, July 1991), pp. 22-23, citing the Luxembourg Income Study of the U.S., Australia, Britain, Canada, Ger-

many, Israel, the Netherlands, Norway, Sweden, and Switzerland. (Italics in orignial) Also see Mishel and Bernstein, *The State of Working America 1994-95*, pp. 308-19.

12. Campaign for an Effective Crime Policy, *Evaluating Mandatory Minimum Sentences* (Washington, DC, October 1993), p. 5, citing National Conference of State Legislatures, "State Budget and Tax Actions 1993," *City & State*, August 16, 1993.

13. Latino infant mortality rates are higher than for non-Latino Whites and lower than for Blacks. The Black-White infant mortality gap is growing. Reuters, "Baby deaths for Blacks 2.5 Times White rate," *Boston Globe*, December 10, 1993; Children's Defense Fund, *Decade of Indifference: Maternal and Child Health Trends* (March 1993 press edition), pp. 7-8, Tables B and C, Table 22 and Joseph Tiang-Yau Liu et al., The Health of America's Children 1992 (Children's Defense Fund, 1992), pp. 12-13.

14. Steven Rattner, "Volcker Asserts U.S. Must Trim Living Standards," *New York Times*, October 18, 1979.

15. Mishel and Bernstein, *The State of Working America 1994-95*, pp. 71-74, 188-91. Also see "Spiraling down: The fall of real wages," *Dollars & Sense*, April 1992.

16. Children's Defense Fund, *Vanishing Dreams*, pp. 2-3, 10-17, 23, Tables in Appendix.

17. Mishel and Bernstein, *The State of Working America 1994-95*, pp. 108-13, 137.

18. Jeremy Rifkin, *The End of Work* (New York: Jeremy P. Tarcher/Putnam, 1995), p. 91.

19. "The Real Truth About the Economy," *Business Week*, November 7, 1994, pp. 113, 116.

20. Myron Magnet, "The Productivity Payoff Arrives," *Fortune*, June 27, 1994.

21. Jaclyn Fierman, "When Will You Get a Raise?" *Fortune*, July 12, 1993.

22. Census Bureau, "The Earnings Ladder: Who's at the Bottom? Who's at the Top?" *Statistical Brief*, March 1994; *Workers With Low Earnings: 1964 to 1990* (1992); *Trends in Relative Income: 1964 to 1989* (1991).

23. Richard B. Freeman and Lawrence F. Katz, "Rising Wage Inequality: The United States vs. Other Advanced Countries," in Richard Freeman, ed., *Working Under Different Rules* (New York: Russell Sage Foundation, 1994), p. 30.

24. William E. Spriggs and Bruce W. Klein, *Raising the Floor: The Effects of the Minimum Wage on Low-Wage Workers* (Economic Policy Institute, 1994), pp. 1-4. Data also from Mishel and Bernstein, *The State of Working America 1994-95*, pp. 169-71.

25. Mishel and Bernstein, *The State of Working America 1994-95*, pp. 14-16, 141, 191-95. (Italics in original) Also see Lawrence Mishel and Jared Bernstein, "Declining Wages For High School and College Graduates: Pay and Benefits Trends by Education, Gender, Occupation, and State, 1979-1991," Economic Policy Institute, *Briefing Paper*, May 1992.

26. Mishel and Bernstein, *The State of Working America 1994-95*, p. 198.

27. John Greenwald, "Bellboys with B.A.s," *Time*, November 22, 1993, p. 36.

28. Quote from Labor Research Association, *American Labor Yearbook 1993*, p. 4; Mishel and Bernstein, *The State of Working America 1994-95*, p. 168.

29. Labor Research Association, *American Labor Yearbook 1993*, p. 6.

30. "Why America Needs Unions but Not the Kind It Has Now," *Business Week*, May 23, 1994, p. 78.

31. Labor Research Association, *American Labor Yearbook 1993*, p. 12.

32. George Will, "The Porcelain Presidency," *Newsweek*, July 25, 1994.

33. Labor Research Association, *American Labor Yearbook 1993*, p. 16.

34. "Why America Needs Unions but Not the Kind It Has Now," *Business Week*, pp. 70-71.

35. Commission on the Future of Worker-Management Relations, *Fact Finding Report* (U.S. Department of Labor/U.S. Department of Commerce: May 1994), p. 19. Also

see *The OECD Jobs Study: Facts, Analysis, Strategies* (Paris/Washington, DC: Organization for Economic Cooperation and Development, 1994), pp. 22-23.

36. Labor Research Association, *American Labor Yearbook 1993*, p. 44.

37. *Ibid.*, p. 35.

38. Lance Morrow, "The Temping of America," *Time*, March 29, 1993, pp. 40-41.

39. See, for example, U.S. General Accounting Office (GAO), *Workers At Risk: Increased Numbers in Contingent Employment Lack Insurance, Other Benefits* (March 1991); Janice Castro, "Disposable Workers," *Time*, March 29, 1993; S. C. Gwynne, "The Long Haul," *Time*, September 28, 1992; Bruce D. Butterfield, " 'Leasing' employees: a growing discount service," *Boston Globe*, March 21, 1993; Camille Colatosi, "A Job without a Future," *Dollars & Sense*, May 1992; Peter T. Kilborn, "A Disrupting Change Hits Workers After Recession," *New York Times*, December 26, 1992.

40. "Business Gives in to Temptation," *U.S. News & World Report*, July 4, 1994. Also see "The New Migrant Workers," in the same issue.

41. Lawrence Mishel and Jared Bernstein, "The Joyless Recovery: Deteriorating Wages and Job Quality in the 1990s, Economic Policy Institute *Briefing Paper*, September 1993, pp. 2, 15-16, 20.1979-89 figures from Mishel and Bernstein, *The State of Working America 1994-95*, pp. 151-55, 220-21.

42. Kenneth C. Crowe, *Newsday*, "Full-Time Workers vs. the Part-Timers: A New Battleground," *Philadelphia Inquirer*, June 1, 1994.

43. Mishel and Bernstein, *The State of Working America 1994-95*, pp. 221-23, and Bruce D. Butterfield, "Diminished Jobs, Added Worry," *Boston Globe*, March 21, 1993.

44. Castro, "Disposable Workers," pp. 43-47.

45. *Left Business Observer*, No. 61, December 13, 1993.

46. On global corporate strategies and long-term planning, see Holly Sklar, ed., *Trilateralism: The Trilateral Commission and Elite Planning for World Management* (Boston: South End Press, 1980).

47. Quote from Richard J. Barnet and John Cavanagh, *Global Dreams: Imperial Corporations and the New World Order* (New York: Simon & Schuster, 1994), p. 275. Also see *Left Business Observer*, No. 61, December 13, 1993.

48. Lois Marie Gibbs and Pamela K. Stone, "Corporate Tax Breaks: The Real Welfare Scam," in *Everyone's Backyard* (Center for Environmental Justice, Citizens Clearinghouse for Hazardous Waste: 1992), p. 3, cited in Eva Gladstein, "Livelihoods in Jeopardy," AFSC working paper, 1994.

49. Robert Goodman, *The Last Entrepreneurs: America's Regional Wars for Jobs and Dollars* (Boston: South End Press, 1982), p. 4.

50. Rebecca Smith and Thomas Farragher, "Why California Lost in Bid for Intel Plant," *San Jose Mercury News*, April 4, 1993.

51. "Europe: The Push East," *Business Week*, November 7, 1994, p. 48.

52. Charles T. Jones, "Temp Worker Agencies See Need for Better-Prepared U.S. Workforce," *The Daily Oklahoman*, October 31, 1994.

53. Paul Lima, *Computer Dealer News* (Canada), June 1, 1994.

54. Edward A. Gargan, "India Among the Leaders in Software for Computers," *New York Times*, December 29, 1993.

55. "The Mexican Worker: Smart, Motivated, Cheap," *Business Week*, April 19, 1993. Also see Harley Shaiken, "Advanced Manufacturing and Mexico" *Latin American Research Review* 29:2, 1994. Mexican minimum wage and productivity figures from Richard Rothstein, "Who Will Buy?" *CEO/International Strategies*, December 1993/January 1994, p. 24. *Wall Street Journal* cite from Sarah Anderson and John Cavanagh, "The NAFTA Alternative," op-ed distributed by the Progressive Media Project.

56. See Annette Fuentes and Barbara Ehrenreich, *Women in the Global Factory* (Boston: South End Press, 1983) and Rachel Kamel, *The Global Factory* (Philadelphia: American Friends Service Committee, 1990).

57. Charles Kernaghan, The National Labor Committee in Support of Worker and Human Rights in Central America, *Paying to Lose Our Jobs* (New York: September 1992), pp. 54-55.

58. Charles Kernaghan, The National Labor Committee in Support of Worker and Human Rights in Central America, *Free Trade's Hidden Secrets: Why We Are Losing Our Shirts* (New York: November 1993), pp. 1-2, Appendix 1.

59. Ted Plafker, "Brown, in China, Stresses Trade over Rights," *Boston Globe*, August 30, 1994.

60. Joseph Pereira, "Split Personality: Social Responsibility and Need for Low Cost Clash at Stride Rite," *Wall Street Journal*, May 28, 1993.

61. Laurie Udesky, "The 'Social Responsibility' Gap: Sweatshops Behind the Labels," *The Nation*, May 16, 1994. Also see letters exchange, August 8/15, 1994.

62. Rothstein, "Who Will Buy?" p. 25.

63. Bennett Harrison, *Lean and Mean: The Changing Landscape of Corporate Power in the Age of Flexibility* (New York: Basic Books, 1994), p. 205.

64. Jacqueline Jones, *The Dispossessed: America's Underclasses from the Civil War to the Present* (New York: Basic Books, 1992), p. 289.

65. Census Bureau, *Statistical Abstract of the United States 1993* (hereafter *Statistical Abstract* with year), Tables 625, 629, 635.

66. Edward S. Herman, "The Natural Rate of Unemployment," *Z Magazine*, November 1994, p. 64.

67. Labor Research Association, *American Labor Yearbook 1993*, p. 35.

68. "Hats Off! It was a Heck of a Year," *Fortune*, April 18, 1994, pp. 210-13.

69. "Hot Damn! They Did It Again" and "What's Making Those Margins So Fat?" *Business Week*, November 14, 1994.

70. American Management Association, *1994 AMA Survey on Downsizing and Assistance to Displaced Workers* (New York: 1994), p. 7 and "Summary of Key Findings," p. 4.

71. "The New World of Work," *Business Week*, October 17, 1994, p. 85.

72. Schor, *The Overworked American*, pp. 154-55; Rifkin, *The End of Work*, pp. 25-29.

73. American Management Association, *1994 AMA Survey*, p. 5.

74. Juliet Schor, "A Sustainable Economy for the Twenty-First Century," paper prepared for the New Party, July 1994. Also see Schor, *The Overworked American: The Unexpected Decline of Leisure* (New York: Basic Books, 1991).

75. Adam Levy, "Overtime Wearing Thin Across the U.S.," *Philadelphia Inquirer*, October 4, 1994. Also see George J. Church, "We're #1 and It Hurts," *Time*, October 24, 1994.

76. "The New World of Work," *Business Week*, October 17, 1994, p. 87.

77. David Bacon, "Another Sellout of the Workers? Labor Law 'Reform,' " *The Nation*, May 30, 1994.

78. "The Real Truth About the Economy," *Business Week*, November 7, 1994, pp. 110-11.

79. Robert D. Hershey Jr., "Jobless Rate Underestimated, U.S. Says, Citing Survey Bias," *New York Times*, November 17, 1993. While useful for reporting the gender bias, this article misrepresents the impact of the change in the discouraged worker category.

80. David Dembo and Ward Morehouse, *The Underbelly of the U.S. Economy: Joblessness and the Pauperization of Work in America* (New York: Council on International

and Public Affairs, 1994), pp. 7-17, 41-46. Also see *Statistical Abstract 1993*, Table 657.

81. Data from U.S. House of Representatives, Committee on Ways and Means, *1994 Green Book: Overview of Entitlement Programs* (hereafter *Green Book* with year), July 1994, p. 1096. Quote from Mishel and Bernstein, *State of Working America 1994-95*, p. 202.

82. Patricia Kirkpatrick, "Triple Jeopardy: Disability, Race and Poverty in America," *Poverty & Race*, Poverty & Race Research Action Council, Washington, DC, May/June 1994.

83. John M. McNeil, *Americans With Disabilities: 1991-92*, Census Bureau, December 1993, p. 12 and Table 24.

84. *1994 Green Book*, p. 1102. GAO, *Unemployment Insurance: Program's Ability to Meet Objectives Jeopardized*, September 1993. Only one out of three of the official unemployed received benefits on average from 1984 to 1989; the figure rose to 42 percent in 1991 and 52 percent in 1992, still much less than the 76 percent who received benefits during the 1975 recession. The figure dropped to 48 percent in 1993. Isaac Shapiro and Marion Nichols, *Far From Fixed: An Analysis of the Unemployment Insurance System* (Center on Budget and Policy Priorities, March 1992), pp. 1-7, 16; *1994 Green Book*, pp. 266-67, 1102; *1993 Green Book*, pp. 490-523.

85. Shapiro and Nichols, *Far From Fixed*, p. 25. Also see Iris J. Lav et al., *The States and the Poor: How Budget Decisions Affected Low Income People in 1992* (Center on Budget and Policy Priorities/Center for the Study of the States, 1993).

86. "The New World of Work," *Business Week*, October 17, 1994, p. 80.

87. Quoted in Martin Khor, "Worldwide unemployment will reach crisis proportions, says social expert," Third World Network, *Briefings for the Social Summit*, No. 9, August 1994.

88. Rifkin, *The End of Work*, p. 109.

89. Judis, "Why Your Wages Keep Falling."

90. Gary Blonston, "Workers' role in '90s efficiency," *Philadelphia Inquirer*, August 8, 1993.

91. Gretchen Morgenson, "The Fall of the Mall," *Forbes*, May 24, 1993.

92. Paul Lima, *Computer Dealer News* (Canada), June 1, 1994.

93. Rifkin, *The End of Work*, pp. 81-82.

94. *Ibid.*, pp. 261-62.

95. Children's Defense Fund, *Vanishing Dreams*, p. 10. (Italics in original)

96. Schwarz and Volgy, *The Forgotten Americans*, p. 11.

97. Jon Meacham, "Down and Out," *The Washington Monthly*, November 1993, p. 26.

98. Mead quoted in Richard A. Cloward and Frances Fox Piven, "The Fraud of Workfare," *The Nation*, May 24, 1993. Mishel and Bernstein, *The State of Working America 1994-95*, pp. 272, 277-93.

99. Lynne Duke, "But Some of My Best Friends Are. . . ," *Washington Post Weekly*, January 14-20, 1991.

100. Coramae Richey Mann, *Unequal Justice: A Question of Color* (Bloomington, IN: Indiana University Press, 1993), p. 33, citing R. L. McNeely and Carl E. Pope, *Race, Crime and Criminal Justice* (Beverly Hills, CA: Sage Publications, 1981).

101. Thomas H. O'Connor, "A city of 'foreigners': then and now," *Boston Globe*, January 24, 1993. On the Massachusetts registry, see Dolores Kong, "Vital records speak volumes on tougher times," *Boston Globe*, December 27, 1992.

102. Black per capita income was 59 percent of White in 1993; Latino income was 53 percent of White. Census Bureau, *Income, Poverty, and Valuation of Noncash Ben-

efits: 1993, prepublication press excerpts (October 1994).

103. David Cole, "The New Know-Nothingism: Five Myths About Immigration," *The Nation,* October 17, 1994, citing a 1994 report by the Urban Institute and studies cited by the 1994 ACLU Immigrants' Rights Project report; and see Elizabeth Kadetsky, " 'Save Our State' Initiative: Bashing Illegals in California"; Leslie Marmon Silko, "America's Iron Curtain: The Border Patrol State"; and Peter Kwong, "Wake of the Golden Venture: China's Human Traffickers," in the same issue of *The Nation.* Also see Ashley Dunn, "Greeted at Nation's Front Door, Many Visitors Stay on Illegally," *New York Times,* January 3, 1995.

104. Author's conversation with Mimi Abramovitz, December 23, 1992. Also see, for example, Patricia Hill Collins, *Black Feminist Thought* (New York: Routledge, 1991) and Susan Faludi, *Backlash* (New York: Crown, 1991).

105. See Holly Sklar, "The Upperclass and Mothers N the Hood," *Z Magazine,* March 1993.

106. For women the greatest threat of violent injury and death is from so-called "domestic violence" by past or present spouses or boyfriends, which "is the leading cause of injury to women and accounts for more visits to hospital emergency departments than car crashes, muggings, and rapes combined." About a third of all murdered women are killed by husbands, boyfriends, and ex-partners (less than a tenth are killed by strangers)—"men commonly kill their female partners in response to the woman's attempt to leave an abusive relationship." Arthur L. Kellermann and James A. Mercy, "Men, Women, and Murder: Gender-Specific Differences in Rates of Fatal Violence and Victimization," *The Journal of Trauma* 33:1, July 1992. In the words of a congressional report, "Every week is a week of terror for at least 21,000 American women" of all races, regions, and economic backgrounds, whose "domestic assaults, rapes, and murders were reported to the police." Up to 3 million domestic violence crimes may go unreported yearly. U.S. Senate Judiciary Committee, *Violence Against Women: A Week in the Life of America,* prepared by the Majority Staff, October 1992, pp. ix, 1-3.

107. "Shalala Speaks on Teen Mothers," *Boston Globe,* July 15, 1994; Judith Stacey, "Dan Quayle's Revenge: The New Family Values Crusaders," *The Nation,* July 25/ August 1, 1994.

108. Ricki Solinger, *Wake Up Little Susie: Single Pregnancy and Race Before Roe v. Wade* (New York: Routledge, 1992), pp. 41, 148.

109. Stephanie Coontz, *The Way We Never Were: American Families and the Nostalgia Trap* (New York: Basic, 1993), p. 223; also see pp. 221-28. Coontz critiques Judith Wallerstein's famous study of children of divorced parents.

110. At least 80 percent "of the increase in single parents between 1981 and 1983 is attributable to technical refinements in survey procedures that were introduced early in the 1980s. This represents 10 to 15 percent of the total increase between 1970 and 1993 (or 20 to 25 percent of the increase since 1980)." Steve W. Rawlings, Census Bureau, *Household and Family Characteristics: March 1993* (June 1994), pp. vi-vii, xiv-xviii.

111. The 1990 birth rate of unmarried (never-married, divorced, widowed) Black women is higher than it was in 1980, but lower than it was in 1970 (the birth rates of unmarried White women have risen steadily). Also, the overall percentage of total births to teenage mothers was actually less in 1990 than 1980. GAO, *Poverty Trends, 1980-88: Changes in Family Composition and Income Sources Among the Poor* (September 1992), pp. 4, 35-38, 40-43, 53; *Statistical Abstract 1993,* Tables 101-102; *1993 Green Book,* pp. 1138-1146. Also see Mishel and Bernstein, *The State of Working America*

1994-95, pp. 272-76.

112. *1992 Green Book*, pp. 1086-87; Arlene F. Saluter, Census Bureau, *Marital Status and Living Arrangements: March 1993* (May 1994), pp.VII-IX, Table 8. The Census Bureau count of same-sex partners with and without children is considered very low.

113. GAO, *U.S. Has Made Slow Progress in Involving Women in Development*, December 1993, pp. 53, 56, citing, for example, Rae Lesser Blumberg, *Making the Case by the Gender Variables: Women and the Wealth and Well-Being of Nations* (Washington, DC: 1989). United Nations Children's Fund (UNICEF), *The Progress of Nations* (New York: 1993), pp. 41, 43.

114. Quote in *1993 Green Book*, p. 1116; data, *Statistical Abstract 1994*, Table 1358. Also see *1992 Green Book*, pp. 1077, 1288-1300.

115. Census Bureau, Table L, "Poverty Status of Families, by Type of Family, Presence of Related Children, Race, and Hispanic Origin: 1959 to 1993."

116. Labor Research Association, *American Labor Yearbook 1993*, p. 38.

117. Karin Stallard, Barbara Ehrenreich, and Holly Sklar, *Poverty in the American Dream: Women and Children First* (Boston: South End Press, 1983), p. 9, citing, Patricia C. Sexton, *Women and Work*, R. and D. Monograph No. 46, U.S. Department of Labor, Employment and Training Administration (1977).

118. GAO, *Mother-Only Families: Low Earnings Will Keep Many Children in Poverty* (April 1991), pp. 3, 6. Also see Heidi Hartmann et al., "Raising Wages: The Family Issue of the 90's," *Equal Means*, Winter 1991.

119. Census Bureau, *Household and Family Characteristics: March 1993*, Tables B and 15.

120. *1994 Green Book*, pp. 706-7; GAO, *Tax Expenditures Deserve More Scrutiny* (June 1994), p. 50. In 1991, about 81 percent of the $37 billion in tax benefits from deductible mortgage interest went to the top 20 percent of households with incomes above $50,000. See Edward B. Lazere, Paul. A. Leonard, Cushing N. Dolbeare, and Barry Zigas, *A Place to Call Home: The Low Income Housing Crisis Continues* (Center on Budget and Policy Priorities/Low Income Housing Information Service, December 1991), pp. 27, 30-31, 34-35.

121. The Boston Foundation Carol R. Goldberg Seminar on Child Care, *Embracing Our Future: A Child Care Action Agenda* (Boston: Boston Foundation, 1992), pp. 39, 54-5; Children's Defense Fund, *State of America's Children 1992*, pp. 18-22; Barbara Presley Noble, "Worthy Child-Care Pay Scales," *New York Times*, April 18, 1993; Child Care Employee Project, *The National Child Care Staffing Study Revisited: Four Years in the Life of Center-Based Child Care* (Oakland, CA: 1993).

122. The Boston Foundation, *Embracing Our Future*, p. 31.

123. Rosemary L. Bray, "So How Did I Get Here?" *New York Times Magazine*, November 8, 1992.

124. Unemployment rate from *Statistical Abstract 1993*, Table 652. Other data from *1994 Green Book*, pp. 390, 399-403.

125. Barbara Presley Noble, "An Increase in Bias Is Seen Against Pregnant Workers," *New York Times*, January 2, 1993; "Women, Children and Work," *New York Times* editorial, January 12, 1993. Health insurance study in Robert Moffitt and Barbara Wolfe, "The Effect of the Medicaid Program on Welfare Participation and Labor Supply," National Bureau of Economic Research, Working Paper N. 3286 (Cambridge, MA: 1990), cited in GAO, *Mother-Only Families*, p. 6, fn. 7.

126. Jordana Hart, "Few in Area Use Leave Law, Parents Can't Afford Time Off," *Boston Globe*, July 22, 1994.

127. There is no federally prescribed minimum for the AFDC benefit which is set by

states. The median monthly benefit for a family of three in 1994 was $366, which at $4,392 a year, is much less than that year's official poverty threshold for a single individual. *1994 Green Book*, pp. 231, 374-77; Lav et al., *The States and the Poor*, pp. 11-14; also see House Ways and Means Committee, *Background Material on Family Income and Benefit Changes*, pp. 7-8.

128. Paul A. Leonard and Edward B. Lazere, *A Place To Call Home: The Low Income Housing Crisis In 44 Major Metropolitan Areas* (Center on Budget and Policy Priorities, November 1992), pp. 1, 5-8, 36-41; *1993 Green Book*, p. 712; U.S. Department of Health and Human Services (HHS), *Characteristics and Financial Circumstances of AFDC Recipients: FY 1990*, p. 8.

129. GAO, *Poverty Trends, 1980-88*, p. 52. "In 1972, all States paid AFDC benefits to a family with wages equal to 75 percent of the poverty threshold; by 1991, only 5 states paid AFDC to such a family. Average tax rates on such earnings increased from 52 to 69 percent from 1972 to 1984, and then fell to 56 percent in 1991." House Ways and Means Committee, *Background Material on Family Income and Benefit Changes*, pp. 7-8, 36.

130. Harvard School of Public Health, Henry J. Kaiser Family Foundation and KRC, "National Election Night Survey," November 1994.

131. Catherine Lerza, "Sex, Lies & Welfare Reform," *Equal Means*, Spring 1992; Robin Toner, "Politics of Welfare: Focusing on the Problems," *New York Times*, July 5, 1992. Also see, for example, Nancy Gibbs, "The War on Welfare Mothers?" *Time* cover story, June 20, 1994; "Endangered Family," *Newsweek*, August 30, 1993 and Brian McGrory, "Sharp rise in births to unmarried Whites stirs welfare worries," *Boston Globe*, January 3, 1994.

132. The *1993 Green Book* explains variations among different measures of length of time on welfare and why, though (over time) most recipients are short term recipients, at any one point in time there will be a large proportion of long-term recipients on the rolls. See pp. 685-97, 699, 705, 708, 714-18. Also see HHS, *Characteristics and Financial Circumstances of AFDC Recipients: FY 1992*. Most families on AFDC have one child (42 percent) or two children (30 percent); only 10 percent have more than three children.

133. HHS, *Characteristics and Financial Circumstances of AFDC Recipients FY 1992*, pp. 42-43; *1993 Green Book*, pp. 696-98, 706, 727-28.

134. *1993 Green Book*, pp. 721-23. Not surprisingly, though, given impoverished schools, etc., a higher percentage of daughters who were on welfare receive it as young adults than those who weren't.

135. In 1900, Black women's labor force participation rate was 40.7 percent, White women's 16 percent. The 1960 rates were 42.2 percent for Black women and 33.6 percent for Whites; in 1970, 49.5 percent and 42.6 percent; in 1980, 53.2 percent and 51.2 percent; and in 1991 they converged at nearly 58 percent. Teresa L. Amott and Julie A. Matthaei, *Race, Gender & Work* (Boston: South End Press, 1991), Appendix C, Table C-1; *Statistical Abstract 1992*, Table 609.

136. Census Bureau, Table L, "Poverty Status of Families, by Type of Family, Presence of Related Children, Race, and Hispanic Origin: 1959 to 1993." Many women leave welfare—though often not poverty—after finding jobs and/or marrying men. See Coontz, *The Way We Never Were*, pp. 262 and 367-68, fn. 17, on the biased reporting of women "marrying out" of welfare, even if they left because of a job and only later married.

137. Alison Mitchell, "Posing as Welfare Recipient, Agency Head Finds Indignity," *New York Times*, February 5, 1993.

138. 1988 federal study cited in Children's Defense Fund, "Myths About AFDC," *The State of America's Children 1992*, p. 31; child care exemptions, p. 20. Work exemption figures and children's ages from HHS, *Characteristics and Financial Circumstances of AFDC Recipients: FY 1990*, pp. 2, 5. A study of welfare recipients found that four out of ten recipients work at paid jobs, either by simultaneously combining work and welfare benefits (17 percent) or cycling between work and welfare (22 percent). Roberta M. Spalter-Roth, Heidi I. Hartmann, and Linda Andrews, *Combining Work and Welfare: An Alternative Anti-Poverty Strategy*, A Report to the Ford Foundation (Washington, DC: Institute for Women's Policy Research, 1992). Also see the Institute for Women's Policy Research reports, *The Real Employment Opportunities of Women Participating in AFDC: What the Market Can Provide* (October 1993) and *Dependence on Men, the Market, or the State: The Rhetoric and Reality of Welfare Reform* (November 1993).

139. Schwarz and Volgy, "Above the Line—But Poor."

140. Jonathan Kozol, *Savage Inequalities: Children in America's Schools* (New York: Crown Publishers, 1991).

141. Jeff P. Howard, "The Third Movement: Developing Black Children for the 21st Century," in National Urban League, *The State of Black America 1993* (New York: 1993), pp. 20-21.

142. Jean Caldwell, "Ending Tracking: Difficult and Controversial," *Boston Globe*, November 14, 1993.

143. Deborah Prothrow-Stith, *Deadly Consequences: How Violence is Destroying Our Teenage Population and a Plan to Begin Solving the Problem* (New York: Harper Perennial, 1991/1993), pp. 164-66, 169-71.

144. Robert Kominski and Andrea Adams, Census Bureau, *Educational Attainment in the United States: March 1993 and 1992* (May 1994), Table 2.

145. "Inequality: How the Gap Between Rich and Poor Hurts the Economy," *Business Week*, August 15, 1994, p. 79. Congressional commission cited in Mary Jordan, *Washington Post*, "Panel to call for new student-aid system," *Boston Globe*, February 3, 1993. Associated Press, "US college costs still rising faster than income," *Boston Globe*, September 22, 1993.

146. Judith Gaines, "Work, study: High costs shift college priorities," *Boston Globe*, September 16, 1994.

147. People for the American Way, *Democracy's Next Generation II: A Study of American Youth on Race* (Washington, DC: 1992), pp. 41, 161. Also see Lynne Duke, "Just When You Thought It Was the 20th Century. . . ," *Washington Post Weekly*, January 6-12, 1992; Tom W. Smith, "Ethnic Images in the United States," *The Polling Report* 7:11, May 27, 1991.

148. Diane E. Lewis, "Employment testing: Useful tool, or entrapment?" *Boston Globe*, April 11, 1993.

149. Mishel and Bernstein, *The State of Working America 1994-95*, pp. 185-86.

150. Margery Austin Turner et al., *Opportunities Denied, Opportunities Diminished: Racial Discrimination in Hiring*, (Washington, DC: Urban Institute Press, 1991), pp. 2, 56-57.

151. Between July 1990 and March 1991, Blacks were the only racial group to suffer a net loss in jobs at companies that provide employment statistics to the Equal Employment Opportunity Commission. Elaine Ray, "Another Depression," *Boston Globe*, September 24, 1993 and Meg Vaillancourt, "Figures show large job loss among Blacks," *Boston Globe*, September 15, 1993, citing *Wall Street Journal* study. *Wall Street Journal* quote from Acel Moore, "Recession Hit Blacks the Hardest—Why is that Not

Surprising?" *Philadelphia Inquirer*, September 28, 1993.

152. Editorial, "Federal Racism: Blacks are Fired from Jobs at a Higher Rate than Whites," *San Jose Mercury News*, October 26, 1994. Also see "Race and the Workplace: A Study of Firings Raises Old Questions Anew," editorial, *Philadelphia Inquirer*, December 18, 1993; Stephen Barr, "The Shrinking Federal Work Force," *Washington Post Weekly*, September 19-25, 1994.

153. Anne B. Fisher, "When Will Women Get To The Top?" *Fortune*, September 21, 1992, p. 45. Also see "Corporate Women: Progress?," *Business Week*, June 8, 1992; Judith H. Dobrzynski, "The 'Glass Ceiling,': A Barrier to the Boardroom, Too," *Business Week*, November 22, 1993; U.S. Labor Department, *Report on the Glass Ceiling Initiative*, 1991. Survey of executives reported in Ellis Cose, "To the Victors, Few Spoils," *Newsweek*, March 29, 1993, p. 54; also David Gates, "White Male Paranoia," in the same issue.

154. Times Mirror Center for The People & The Press, "The People, the Press & Politics: The New Political Landscape," News Release, September 21, 1994.

155. Hubert Williams and Patrick V. Murphy, "The Evolving Strategy of Police: A Minority View," *Perspectives on Policing*, U.S. Department of Justice (January 1990), p. 2.

156. *New York Times* editorial, "Young Black Men," May 7, 1992.

157. Marc Mauer, *Americans Behind Bars: The International Use of Incarceration, 1992-1993* (Washington, DC: The Sentencing Project, September 1994).

158. U.S. Department of Justice, Bureau of Justice Statistics, *Criminal Victimization in the United States: 1973-92 Trends*, A National Crime Victimization Survey Report, July 1994; *Criminal Victimization in the United States, 1992*, March 1994; *Highlights from 20 Years of Surveying Crime Victims: The National Crime Victimization Survey, 1973-92*, October 1993.

159. Racial composition figures from Bureau of Justice Statistics, *Prisoners in 1993* (June 1994); Caroline Wolf Harlow, Bureau of Justice Statistics, *Comparing Federal and State Prison Inmates* (September 1994); Craig Perkins, Bureau of Justice Statistics, *National Corrections Reporting Program, 1992* (October 1994), p. 83; *Survey of State Prison Inmates, 1991* (March 1993). Also see Patrick A. Langan, Bureau of Justice Statistics, *Race of Prisoners Admitted to State and Federal Institutions, 1926-86* (May 1991).

160. The 1989 figures for women were 1 in 37 Blacks, 1 in 56 Latinas, and 1 in 100 Whites. Mark Mauer, *Young Black Men and the Criminal Justice System* (The Sentencing Project, 1990); Mauer, *Americans Behind Bars: The International Use of Incarceration*.

161. Jerome C. Miller, *Hobbling A Generation: Young African American Males In Washington, DC's Criminal Justice System* (Alexandria, VA: National Center on Institutions and Alternatives, April 17, 1992), pp. 1, 5; National Center on Institutions and Alternatives, *Hobbling a Generation: Baltimore, Maryland* (September 1992), pp. 1-4.

162. Mike Davis, *City of Quartz: Excavating the Future in Los Angeles* (New York: Vintage, 1990), p. 284, citing *Los Angeles Times*, May 8, 1988. Gates has also said that a disproportionate number of Blacks died as a result of police chokeholds because they didn't have veins in their necks "like normal people." See Mann, *Unequal Justice*, p. 152.

163. Carol Stocker and Barbara Carton, "GUILTY. . . of being Black," *Boston Globe*, May 7, 1992. Also see Peter Medoff and Holly Sklar, *Streets of Hope: The Fall and Rise of an Urban Neighborhood* (Boston: South End Press, 1994), chapter 8; Sklar, "Young and Guilty By Stereotype," *Z Magazine*, July/August 1993; and ABC News,

20/20, "Presumed Guilty," November 6, 1992, on Los Angeles.
164. Mann, *Unequal Justice*, pp. 167-71, 181-84, 213-14.
165. *Ibid.*, p. 188, citing Joan Petersilia, "Racial Disparities in the Criminal Justice System," *Crime and Delinquency* 31:1, 1985.
166. The U.S. Department of Health and Human Services, National Institute on Drug Abuse (NIDA) produces regular detailed surveys on drug use. On biased drug wars, past and present, see, for example, Steven B. Duke and Albert C. Gross, *America's Longest War: Rethinking Our Tragic Crusade Against Drugs* (New York: Jeremy P. Tarcher/Putnam, 1993); Diana R. Gordon, *The Return of the Dangerous Classes: Drug Prohibition and Policy Politics* (New York: W.W. Norton & Co., 1994); Mann, *Unequal Justice*, pp. 58-62.
167. Drugs and Crime Data Center, Bureau of Justice Statistics, *Drugs and Crime Facts, 1993* (August 1994); *Statistical Abstract 1993*, Table 316; FBI, *Crime in the United States 1991: Uniform Crime Reports* (August 1992), p. 231 and FBI, *Crime in the United States 1992* (October 1993), p. 235; Bureau of Justice Statistics, *Survey of State Prison Inmates, 1991*; U.S. Department of Justice statisticians, citing 1993 federal statistics; Mauer, *Americans Behind Bars: One Year Later* (The Sentencing Project, February 1992), p. 7, citing *Washington Post*, April 25, 1991; *The World Almanac and Book of Facts 1993* (New York: Pharos Books, 1992), p. 950.
168. Gordon, *The Return of the Dangerous Classes*, p. 143.
169. American Bar Association, Section of Criminal Justice, *The State of Criminal Justice* (Chicago: ABA, February 1993), pp. ii, 11.
170. Special Series, "Is the Drug War Racist?" Sam Vincent Meddis, "Disparities Suggest the Answer Is Yes," *USA Today*, July 23-25, 1993; also see other articles in series.
171. Ira J. Chasnoff, et al., "The Prevalence of Illicit-Drug or Alcohol Use During Pregnancy and Discrepancies in Mandatory Reporting in Pinellas County, Florida," *New England Journal of Medicine*, April 26, 1990, pp. 1202-06.
172. United States Sentencing Commission, Special Report to the Congress, *Mandatory Minimum Penalties in the Federal Criminal Justice System*, Washington, DC, August 1991, pp. ii, 10, 50-54, 76, 82, 91, 107, Appendix A. Also see Lois G. Forer, *A Rage to Punish: The Unintended Consequences of Mandatory Sentencing* (New York: W.W. Norton, 1994); Forer is a former judge.
173. The federal mandatory minimum of five years applies to distribution of 500 grams of powder cocaine, but as little as 5 grams of crack cocaine—nine out of ten persons sentenced for federal crack offenses in 1992 were Black. (In 1990, 500 grams of powder cocaine was worth about $50,000; 5 grams of crack, about $125). There is also a 5-year mandatory minimum for simple possession of more than 5 grams of crack (the same minimum, for example, as a second offense for the sexual exploitation of children). In 1991, the Minnesota Supreme Court declared unconstitutional state statutes mandating a sentence of four years in prison for a first-time conviction for possession of 3 grams of crack, but probation for first-time possession of 3 grams of powder cocaine. The evidence showed that in 1988, over 92 percent of all persons convicted of crack possession were Black while 85 percent of those convicted of powder cocaine possession were White. The court found there is no rational basis for distinguishing between crack cocaine and powder cocaine. U.S. Sentencing Commission, *Mandatory Minimum Penalties*, pp. 9, 31; Campaign For An Effective Crime Policy, "Evaluating Mandatory Minimum Sentences," October 1993, p. 4, citing Dennis Cauchon, "Sentences for Crack Called Racist," *USA Today*, May 26, 1993; Clarence Lusane, *Pipe Dream Blues: Racism and the War on Drugs* (Boston: South End Press, 1991), pp. 44-46; United States Code, Title 21, Sections 841 and 844 (drug offenses

and penalties). On Minnesota case, see Mauer, *Americans Behind Bars: One Year Later*, p. 12, citing *State v. Russell*, decided December 13, 1991; U.S. Sentencing Commission, *Mandatory Minimum Penalties*, Appendix H-17-19. When crack was introduced it was purposefully marketed to poor inner city neighborhoods, before the suburbs, and one study found that earlier differences in use between Whites and Blacks were related to availability. The rates of current crack use among Blacks, Whites, and Latinos in 1991 were less than 1 percent and past-year use was 1.5 percent or less. Marsha Lillie-Blanton et al., "Probing the Meaning of Racial/Ethnic Group Comparisons in Crack Cocaine Smoking," *Journal of the American Medical Association* 269:8, February 24, 1993; U.S. Department of Health and Human Services, HHS News, December 19, 1991, p. 3, and *NIDA Capsules: Summary of Findings from the 1991 National Household Survey on Drug Abuse*, p. 3.

174. Motor vehicle fatalities are the leading cause of death for people between the ages of 5 and 34—including 40 percent of all teenage deaths—and half of all road deaths are due to drunk drivers. Of the approximately 70,000 deaths due to alcohol and other drug-related overdoses, disease, and injury other than drunk driving road crashes, 64,000 are attributed to alcohol. Cathy Shine and Marc Mauer, *Does the Punishment Fit the Crime? Drug Users and Drunk Drivers: Questions of Race and Class* (The Sentencing Project, March 1993), pp. 4, 6, 11, 17. Also see FBI, *Crime in the United States 1992: Uniform Crime Reports* (October 1993), p. 235; Albert J. Reiss, Jr. and Jeffrey A. Roth, eds., National Research Council, *Understanding and Preventing Violence* (Washington, DC: National Academy Press, 1993), pp. 13-14, 182-203; Prothrow-Stith, *Deadly Consequences*, p. 9; Paul J. Goldstein et al., "Drug-Related Homicide in New York: 1984 and 1988, *Crime and Delinquency* 38:4, October 1992, pp. 467-68, 473; U.S. Department of Justice, *Drugs and Crime Facts, 1991*, pp. 3-7 and *Drugs, Crime, and the Justice System* (December 1992), pp. 5-6, 59; GAO, *The War on Drugs: Arrests Burdening Local Criminal Justice Systems* (April 1991), pp. 2-3, 47.

175. See, for example, the report by Leslie Stahl on CBS, *60 Minutes*, April 11, 1993, which highlighted the overcrowding, early release problem while obscuring the cause and pointing only to solutions such as more prisons and more overcrowding.

176. Vincent Schiraldi, "Trading Books for Bars," *Dollars and Sense*, January-February 1995, p. 43.

177. See Ellen Teninty, "Corporate Taxes: The Return for Our Public Investment," *Equal Means*, Fall 1993.

178. Dan Goodgame, "Welfare for the Well-Off," *Time*, February 22, 1993.

179. Mark Muro, "Class Privilege," *Boston Globe*, September 18, 1991.

180. Coontz, *The Way We Never Were*, p. 69.

181. Thomas F. Jackson, "The State, the Movement, and the Urban Poor: The War on Poverty and Political Mobilization in the 1960s," in Michael B. Katz, ed., *The 'Underclass' Debate: Views from History* (Princeton, NJ: Princeton University Press, 1993), p. 411.

182. Dean Baker, "Generations at War: The Real Problems with Social Security," *Dollars & Sense*, November 1990, p. 16. The gap in White and Black life expectancies widened to seven years as Black life expectancy actually dropped in the 1980s. The life expectancy for Black men in 1991 was 64.6 years while it was 72.9 for White men. The life expectancy for Black women was 73.8 years compared with 79.6 years for White women. *Statistical Abstract 1994*, Table 114, 115.

183. Robert B. Reich, *The Work of Nations* (New York: Alfred A. Knopf, 1991), pp. 199, 260.

184. Refers to federal, state, local expenditures. *Statistical Abstract 1992*, Table 565.

185. The Labor/Community Strategy Center, *Reconstructing Los Angeles From the Bottom Up* (Los Angeles, 1993), p. 41, citing Citizens for Tax Justice.
186. Donald L. Barlett and James B. Steele, *America: Who Really Pays the Taxes?* (New York: Touchstone, 1994), pp. 95-109.
187. As the *Boston Globe* put it in a lengthy series, "As state after state succumbs to the perfume of gambling, the odor of desperation becomes increasingly harder to mask. . . . An exhaustive study by two Duke University economists found that lotteries. . . rather than being a voluntary tax or even a nontax way to balance state budgets. . . prey on the poor and make gamblers of people who never before had placed a bet." Mitchell Zuckoff and Doug Bailey, "US turns to betting as budget fix," *Boston Globe*, September 26, 1993, first of five-part series, "Easy Money; America's Big Gamble."
188. Quote from John Miller, "The Clinton Budget: New Voodoo and Old Snake Oil," *Dollars & Sense*, November/December 1993, p. 32; 1995 figure from Mishel and Bernstein, *The State of Working America 1994-95*, pp. 93-94. See Barlett and Steele, *America: Who Really Pays the Taxes?* on tax-exempt investment, etc..
189. Felicity Barringer, "Giving by the Rich Declines, on Average," *New York Times*, May 24, 1992; *Statistical Abstract 1993*, Table 615.
190. Robert B. Reich, "Secession of the Successful," *New York Times Magazine*, January 20, 1991. Also see *The Work of Nations*.
191. Rep. Maxine Waters, Testimony before the Senate Banking Committee, May 14, 1992.
192. Fact sheet with Children's Defense Fund, *The State of America's Children: Yearbook 1994*. Also see Children's Defense Fund, *The State of America's Children 1992* (Washington, DC: 1992), p. ix.
193. Lynn A. Curtis and Vesta Kimble, *Investing in Children and Youth, Reconstructing Our Cities: Doing What Works to Reverse the Betrayal of American Democracy* (Washington, DC: The Milton S. Eisenhower Foundation, 1993), pp. 12-14, 157-58.
194. Todd Schafer, "Still Neglecting Public Investment: The FY94 Budget Outlook," Economic Policy Institute, *Briefing Paper*, September 1993. Also see Miller, "The Clinton Budget" and Robert Greenstein and Paul Leonard, *A New Direction: The Clinton Budget and Economic Plan* (Center on Budget and Policy Priorities, March 1993).
195. Mishel and Bernstein, *The State of Working America 1994-95*, pp. 325-28.
196. National Priorities Project and Peace Action, *In Search of Security: Reducing America's Military: Rebuilding America's Communities* (Northampton, MA: 1994), p. 2.
197. Center for Defense Information, "Cutting Unnecessary Military Spending: Going Further and Faster," *The Defense Monitor* XXI: 3 (1993) and "Reduce Military Spending: Create More Jobs," *The Defense Monitor* XXIII: 6 (1994).
198. Eyal Press, "Arms Sales and False Economics: Prez Pampers Peddlers of Pain," *The Nation*, October 3, 1994.
199. See, for example, National Priorities Project and Peace Action, *In Search of Security* and Randall Forsberg's articles in the *Boston Review*: "Wasting Billions," April/May 1994; "Creating a Cooperative Security System," November/December 1992; "Defense Cuts and Cooperative Security in the Post-Cold War World, May-July 1992.
200. Muhammad Yunus, "Redefining Development," in Kevin Danaher, ed., *50 Years is Enough: The Case Against the World Bank and the International Monetary Fund* (Boston: South End Press/Global Exchange, 1994).
201. Martin Khor Kok Peng, "Reforming North Economy, South Development, and World Economic Order," in Jeremy Brecher, John Childs and Jill Cutler, eds., *Global Vi-*

sions: *Beyond the New World Order* (Boston: South End Press, 1993), pp. 164-65.

202. UNDP, *Human Development Report 1994*, p. 35.

203. GAO, *U.S. Had Made Slow Progress in Involving Women in Development*, December 1993, pp. 61-62.

204. UNICEF, *The State of the World's Children 1989*, p. 15. Also see UNICEF, *The State of the World's Children 1994*, pp. 50-51.

205. Linda Gray MacKay, "World Bank and IMF Have Failed, and the Poor Pay the Price," *Boston Globe*, July 14, 1994.

206. Quoted in Jeremy Brecher, "Global Village or Global Pillage?," *The Nation*, December 6, 1993.

207. AFSC, *From Global Pillage to Global Village: A Perspective from Working People and People of Color on the Unregulated Internationalization of the Economy and the North American Free Trade Agreement*, October 1993.

208. See, for example, AFSC, *From Global Pillage to Global Village;* Sheila D. Collins, Helen Ginsburg and Gertrude Schaffner Goldberg, *Jobs for All in a Nation That Works* (New York: New Initiatives for Full Employment, 1993); Schor, "A Sustainable Economy for the Twenty-First Century"; Jeremy Brecher and Tim Costello, *Global Village or Global Pillage: Economic Reconstruction from the Bottom Up* (Boston: South End Press, 1994); Brecher, Childs, and Cutler, eds., *Global Visions*; John Cavanagh, Daphne Wysham, and Marcos Arruda, eds., *Beyond Bretton Woods: Alternatives to the Global Economic Order* (Institute for Policy Studies/Pluto Press, 1994); Dan Luria and Joel Rogers, *Metro Futures: A High-Wage, Democratic Development Strategy for America's Cities and Inner Suburbs* (Chicago: Midwest Consortium for Economic Development Alternatives, 1994); The Labor/Community Strategy Center, *Reconstructing Los Angeles From the Bottom Up.*

209. Collins et al., *Jobs for All in a Nation That Works*, p. 62.

210. "Twelve Points to Save the Social Summit," An NGO statement for the second session of the preparatory Committee of the Social Summit, August 25, 1994.

211. Robert Pollin, "Use Conversion to Create Jobs," *The Nation*, July 12, 1993.

212. Terry Collingsworth, J. William Goold, and Pharis J. Harvey, "Time for a Global New Deal," *Foreign Affairs*, January/February 1994, p. 10.

213. The Labor/Community Strategy Center, *Reconstructing Los Angeles From the Bottom Up*, p. 17.

214. Yunus, "Redefining Development," and Jessica Matthews, "Little World Banks," in Danaher, ed., *50 Years is Enough.*

215. See Medoff and Sklar, *Streets of Hope: The Fall and Rise of an Urban Neighborhood.*